THE RIDER

Tim Krabbé

THE RIDER

Translated from the Dutch
by Sam Garrett

BLOOMSBURY

Published by Bloomsbury USA, New York
Distributed to the trade by Holtzbrinck Publishers

The publishers gratefully acknowledge a grant from the
Foundation for the Production and Translation of Dutch Literature.

All papers used by Bloomsbury USA are natural, recyclable products made from wood
grown in well-managed forests. The manufacturing processes conform to the environmental
regulations of the country of origin.

THE LIBRARY OF CONGRESS HAS CATALOGED THE HARDCOVER EDITION AS FOLLOWS:

Krabbé, Tim.
[Renner, English]
The rider / Tim Krabbé ; translated from the Dutch by Sam Garrett.
p. cm.
ISBN 1-58234-203-2
1. Bicycle racing—Fiction. I. Title.

PI5881.21.R26 R4413 2002
819.3'1364—dc21
2001056593

Originally published in Dutch by Uitgeverij Bert Bakker, Amsterdam,
under the title De Renner
First published in the United States by Bloomsbury in 2002
This paperback edition published 2003

Paperback ISBN-10 158234-290-3
ISBN-13 978-1-58234-290-0

7 9 10 8 6

Typeset by Hewer Text Limited, Edinburgh
Printed in Great Britain by Clays Limited, St Ives plc

THE RIDER

Meyrueis, Lozère, June 26, 1977. Hot and overcast. I take my gear out of the car and put my bike together. Tourists and locals are watching from sidewalk cafés. Non-racers. The emptiness of those lives shocks me.

Everywhere cars are parked or driving by with antlers of wheels and frames. A few riders are already pedaling around. Smiling, waving. There are a few I don't know. Good riders? Bad riders? You can tell good riders by their faces, bad riders by their faces too – but that only goes for riders you already know.

I pick up my number at a café, shake a hand on the way back.

'Good legs?'

'We'll see.'

'Haha, right.'

Between the bumper of his car and mine, a rider in a light-blue Cycles Goff jersey is sitting on the curb, deep in thought. Before him on the street lies a back wheel, beside him a wooden box full of sprockets. His gears: he still has to decide which ones to use. There are four cols today, no

I

one knows exactly how steep. I do: I've been over the course.

I don't recognize this guy. We mumble greetings, he muses on. Behind my car I put on my riding gear. Racing shorts, sweatshirt, suspenders, jersey. I toss my street clothes onto the back seat, look at the folds they make when they land. They'll stay that way until I put them on again, or until an official gathers them together after I've died in the race.

Leaning against the fender I eat a banana and a sandwich. Starting time is in forty-five minutes. I want to win this race.

The Tour de Mont Aigoual covers 137 kilometers and loops back twice through Meyrueis. Mont Aigoual is one of the highest peaks in the Cévennes, 1,567 meters. It's on the second loop. The sky out that way is gray. The last descent into Meyrueis crosses the Col de Perjuret, made famous when Roger Rivière broke his back there in 1960.

The Tour de Mont Aigoual is the sweetest, toughest race of the season.

The rider from Cycles Goff picks out six cogs and fastens them to the hub. He nods to himself: the nod of someone closing his final book before an exam.

I peel two oranges, eat half of one, put the rest in the back pocket of my jersey. I fill my bidon with Evian, rinse my hands and lock the car. The keys I give to Stéphan, my spare wheels too. He's driving the support car for my club, the club from Anduze.

I wipe my tires clean and climb onto the bike. From the finish line I retrace the final straightaway. I count the strokes. Forty. That's 250 meters, a long way to sprint out of the curve. Too long? What if I shift up during the sprint? Or is it too short for that?

I cycle the last kilometer. Before the final straightaway are two ninety-degree turns, with only a little bridge in between. If I want to be first into the curves, I'll have to take the lead no later than *here*. At that white sign: CULTE PROTESTANTE, services at ten-thirty every Sunday.

I keep riding till I'm out of Meyrueis. Then I climb off and take a piss. I see two other riders doing the same, a little further along.

No, three.

I look towards Mont Aigoual, at the dark sky, wipe my tires and ride back. Here's where I go to the front. Curve. Curve. Whooosh.

And then one final shift? Maybe I'll come in alone.

Lebusque pulls up next to me in his blue and yellow jersey.

'Muggy,' he says.

'Yeah,' I say.

'Still, it could rain,' he says. He points up.

'Yeah.'

'What gears you using?'

'Fourteen-fifteen-seventeen-eighteen-nineteen-twenty.'

'Oh. I've got thirteen eighteen.'

Lebusque is forty-two. He's big and hulking, easily the strongest man I've ever found myself within arm's reach of.

He looks like the giant who was always throwing Chaplin out of restaurants.

A few riders are already waiting at the start. I look straight into the thick lenses of Barthélemy. We don't greet each other, we're not on speaking terms. Barthélemy is one of the favorites, but put him in the Tour de France and he'd still have the face of a bad rider.

He's talking to Boutonnet, a slim, handsome fellow of thirty with a mean look in his eye. At the start of the season, when the papers reported that Merckx, Maertens and Thurau would be using a number twelve sprocket, Boutonnet rushed off to Italy to buy one. A twelve's what he uses now in our races. He gets teased a little. '*Allez, le douze.*'

There's Reilhan in his green jersey, a nineteen-year-old boy whose soft face is filled with a sense of superiority. Last week I was with him in the decisive break. He took his three strokes out in front, but that was it. And he whipped me in the sprint. He's a good climber too, and he can keep up a steady pace when necessary. What they call a golden boy. Hey there, Reilhan! Wheel-sucker.

I forgot my figs.

Goddamn it, I forgot my figs.

I find Stéphan and ask him for my keys.

'We'll be starting any minute.'

'Give me the keys.'

I cycle over to the car and put three figs in my back pocket. Or should I make it four? Or five? Ballast, I never eat more than two during a race, the others will just end up glistening brown with sweat.

Ballast? But if I think those few extra grams are going to get in my way, I can always eat them, can't I?

Jacques Anquetil, five-time winner of the Tour de France, used to take his water bottle out of its holder before every climb and stick it in the back pocket of his jersey. Ab Geldermans, his Dutch lieutenant, watched him do that for years, until finally he couldn't stand it any more and asked him why. And Anquetil explained.

A rider, said Anquetil, is made up of two parts, a person and a bike. The bike, of course, is the instrument the person uses to go faster, but its weight also slows him down. That really counts when the going gets tough, and in climbing the thing is to make sure the bike is as light as possible. A good way to do that is: take the bidon out of its holder.

So, at the start of every climb, Anquetil moved his water bottle from its holder to his back pocket. Clear enough.

Lebusque is from Normandy, just like Anquetil. He claims to have raced with him twenty-five years ago. And to have come in before him on occasion.

I usually come in before Lebusque.

Lebusque is really only a body. In fact, he's not a good racer. People are made up of two parts: a mind and a body. Of the two, the mind, of course, is the rider. That this mind has recourse to two instruments, a body and a bicycle – both of which have to be as light as possible – doesn't really matter. What Anquetil needed was faith. And nothing is better for a firm and solid faith than being in the wrong.

Jean Graczyk used to cut a potato down the middle every evening and lie down with the two halves on his eyelids. Gabriël Poulain pounded his spokes flat. The Pélissier brothers only trained with the wind at their backs (it sometimes took years for them to get back home). Boutonnet uses a twelve. Coppi had himself carried up the steps of his hotel after every stage of the Tour. Rivière filled his tires with helium. Poulain's wheels collapsed beneath him.

If they'd forbidden Anquetil to put his bidon in his back pocket, he would never have won the Tour de France.

I eat one fig and put four in my back pocket. I pedal up to the start. There are already almost forty riders waiting. Five minutes to starting time.

'Good legs?' the guy beside me asks.

'We'll see. And you?'

He shrugs and starts telling me how little time he has to train. All riders say that, always. As if they're afraid to be judged by that part of their ability they can actually take credit for. 'Guys,' I said one time in the dressing room, 'I've been training my butt off.' There was a shocked, giggly moment of silence, but I was afraid they'd think I was serious.

In front of the start is the loudspeaker car which Roux, the race director, will drive in front of us. We hear the sound of accordions, then Roux's amplified voice cuts in. He tells the crowd that the Tour de Mont Aigoual is an exceptionally hard race, covering 150 kilometers and five cols. He tells us that there are premiums to be won. One hundred, seventy-five and fifty francs for the first three riders making the first pass through Meyrueis, and two others, fifty francs, in Camprieu at the foot of Mont Aigoual.

Kléber is standing in front of me. We greet each other. I point to his bars. 'New tape?'

He smiles apologetically. 'For morale.'

Kléber is my regular training buddy. The two of us checked out the course together. We both like long races with lots of cols. But he rides for Barthélemy's team, and sticks strictly to that during the competition.

I'm standing at the back, but it doesn't matter. I used to think it never mattered. Until race number 145, on August 31, 1974. It was my first really long road race in the Netherlands, the Four-River Tour. A race over 175 kilometers, I figured, so there's no hurry. We rode at a snail's pace through the streets of Tiel, behind the race director's car. Twenty-wide the riders rode, curb-to-curb, without a single gap to move up into. Strange, I thought.

I didn't have a clue.

Outside Tiel the race director waved his flag, I heard the car accelerate, and before I knew what was happening the pack was sprinting as fast as it could. Within ten seconds I had to throw the bike into its highest gear, the one I'd wanted to save for the final hour. The road narrowed. Shouts, curses, scraping, the cracking of spokes. A curve, a rise, we must have been flying up a dyke. In a flash I saw a rider lying crumpled against a post. The world shrank to the pain in my chest and the wheel in front of me. And the wind. That lasted for a few minutes. I passed no one, no one passed me; only by sprinting as hard as I could was I able to stick to the wheel in front of me.

When the pace became less killing for a moment, I looked up. Ten riders in front of me, a huge gap had opened. Twenty riders ahead of that, another. The group had exploded irreparably into three parts. After ten minutes, less than ten kilometers, the race was lost for 100 of the 120 contestants.

Racing customs develop the way dialects do; it seems only Dutch amateur classics start like that.

Do I still have time for a piss? Roux is reading off the names, there's no time left. Fifty-three contestants. A rider is wiping down his tires with his gloves. The mayor of Meyrueis waves his handkerchief. We're off. I've been living for this race for the last six weeks.

○

Kilometer 0–2. People clap goodheartedly. '*Allez, Poupou.*' We leave Meyrueis, behind the accordion. A bang, rattling, a puncture. A rider raises his hand. Deleuze, from Anduze. Goddamn it, there goes a spare wheel.

To the left is the river with its rock wall beyond, to the right more rocks; we're riding through a gorge in the highlands of the Cévennes: the Gorge de la Jonte. The Jonte is the little river flowing clear and innocent beside us.

But still. She once set down these hundred-meter walls of stone.

A *faux plat* going down, the pace picks up right away. I spin along in low gear. My lungs unfold, the air of the canyon blows through my hair, the smell of balsam from other legs spatters off their spokes and into my nostrils. I slide in among the wheels, back and forth, in the continuously shifting braid of the peloton. I'm home again. I started on this sport fifteen years too late.

After one kilometer, a minuscule rider with a black rag-mop attacks: Despuech. Baloney. This race lasts 140 kilometers. Despuech is crazy. Despuech is only showing us that he doesn't stand a chance in hell. He knows it too, but still it's a fact: he has to choose between finishing at the back after shining, or finishing at the back after not having shone at all. Dozens of riders are now thinking the word 'Despuech', and people along the route will clap for him. And later all the riders will slide right over him, like a net over an undersized fish.

In the blink of an eye he's taken fifty meters, a hundred. He's got a nice style, nothing moving except his legs, his hands resting on top of the brakehoods. The road grows curvy, every once in a while he disappears from sight. The peloton couldn't care less. It just crawls along. I'm in the middle of it, my hands up on the bars. In the river below are huge blocks of gray rock. People swimming here and there. Four and a half hours to go.

Kilometer 2–5. A slap on my right buttock. I look to the left. Yes, indeed, it's cheerful old Deleuze again. He's looking rather sweaty.

'Bridged the gap just like that,' he says. He edges past me. Just as I thought: there goes my own spare back wheel, powered by a nobody. Have to tell Stéphan this is way out of line.

Walking speed. The real race hasn't started yet. The first climb won't be for another thirty kilometers, at Les Vignes. I'm longing for it, just like when I'm doing it I'll long for it to be over.

Chatting in the peloton, old acquaintances are being renewed, a guy turns around with no hands on the bars. He gets a scolding. But ever since I saw a rider meticulously peeling a banana with both hands on a downhill stretch at 65 kilometers an hour, I'm no longer afraid of crashes from riding no-hands. You can take a dive any time, of course, but riders can do anything on their bikes. Thirsty racers sometimes even discover that their bidon has been stolen from the holder.

Now Despuech is truly out of sight. Anyone in this bunch could do what Despuech is doing, which isn't to say there's not a certain athletic prowess to it. The speed I keep up effortlessly among the wheels he must exceed on his own.

He has to do without the peloton effect.

In 1898, an American, Hamilton, first pushed the World Hour Record to over forty kilometers. But his achievement was never officially recognized. Why? Because he'd let himself be paced by a dot of light, projected from the field onto the track in front of him. With Hamilton's disqualification, the Union Cycliste Internationale was the first sporting federation to officially recognize the existence of the sportsman's psyche. Even so, that recognition went paired with disapproval – as though Hamilton, by making such overt use of his willpower, had cheated. Ever since then, pacing during record attempts may only take the form of a bell that rings each time the invisible recordholder crosses the line.

That's one aspect of the peloton effect. Greater than the psychological advantage of the pacer, however, is the advantage of his slipstream. I once rode in the North Holland amateur championship, on a course without difficulty or wind, race number 204, on June 1, 1975. For 120 kilometers, a pack of 120 riders stuck together. Up front the cracks drove themselves into the ground to keep up an average of 48 kilometers an hour; at the back the gimps were engrossed in conversation.

The equalizing effect of the slipstream is enormous: I would dare to assert that Merckx himself couldn't have escaped from that bunch. I would also dare to assert that I could have hugged Merckx's wheel when he established his World Hour Record (49.431 km) in Mexico in 1972, but not that I would make it more than forty-one kilometers on my own. Not even if Merckx were on my back wheel, shouting: 'Move it, Krabbé!'

The real world record for the hour, by the way, belongs to a Frenchman, Meiffret, at 109 kilometers. Over shorter distances, this same man reached speeds of more than two hundred kilometers an hour. All behind a pace car with a huge windbreak attached. When he set those records,

Meiffret was well into his sixties and not much of an athlete: a rider like Despuech could have given him the slip any time. Meiffret was able to establish those records only because no one else dared to. They're records in the most literal sense.

Tour de France 1951. Eleventh stage: Brive–Agen, 177 kilometers. A level stage, part of the foreplay to the Tour. And talk about the equalizing effect of the slipstream.

After thirty-four kilometers, Hugo Koblet of Switzerland escaped. This was no Despuech. Koblet was a favorite to win the Tour, which he did, and he had already won a time trial.

For 140 kilometers, over flat, straight roads, the favorite remained in front of the peloton in splendid isolation, finally arriving in Agen with a lead of 2 minutes and 35 seconds.

That kind of thing just doesn't happen.

Here I have a photo of Koblet during that escape. Devil-may-care, graceful tread, hands on top of the bars, a prince goes gliding by. Behind him a broad coalition of rivals is hanging with their noses to the bar, grinding, thrashing themselves to catch up: Coppi, Bartali, Van Est, Bobet, Geminiani, Ockers, Robic. The pursuit continued for more than three hours: to no avail. Every journalist and every photographer being driven along the Tour had plenty of time to pull up and gaze upon this superior creature leading the procession.

I have various photos of Koblet during Brive–Agen, each one showing him stared upon open-mouthed by yet another legend of the past.

At the finish Koblet ran a comb through his hair, and said he'd escaped by accident. There was a little hill just after the start, he'd found himself in the lead there, and when he looked around halfway there was no one on his wheel. So he'd just pressed on, keeping the same rhythm, being careful not to strain himself. 'I guess I was just going faster than the others.'

Nothing like Brive–Agen had ever happened before, and it never happened again. Seeing Koblet ride that year, you could tell that the bicycle had been invented by God himself. But Koblet's career didn't last long. He had feet of clay.

Kilometer 5. Les Gorges de la Jonte. Despuech is nowhere in sight. We're still following the river. Bathers look up, wave, shout something we can't hear. 'Who the hell goes cycling on a hot day like this?'

Five kilometers: Sauveplane escapes. Another idiot. In his yellow-and-white-striped jersey he grinds calmly away from the bunch. He's not really such a bad rider; so why doesn't he just race along with the rest of us? I could do what he's doing, if I wanted to. 'After only five moves, Krabbé made a startling queen sacrifice that had the spectators crowding around his table. After ten moves he resigned.'

No one reacts to Sauveplane's flight. Lebusque, one of the favorites, comes up and rides next to me. I can't make out what he's saying, but I take it he's telling me my own thoughts. 'Sauveplane is crazy.'

Then something even crazier happens. I've escaped too! My reason has to go along, like a ten-year-old boy on a runaway horse. I'm up on the pedals, after five strokes I'm already at top speed, the oxygen shouts hurrah down to my finest blood vessels, there I go hammering past the pack, past the point rider, out into space. Behind me they're shouting: 'Ho hey, ho hey.' In front of me is Sauveplane. Without touching my gears, right on the tip of the saddle, my torso at least ten degrees off my frame and I've got him. It seems like I haven't even had enough time to breathe. I stop pedaling, end up right on his wheel and feel a silly laugh in my lungs and calves.

Now I'm staring at Sauveplane's backside. He's strong as an ox, but ugly, a stamping bruiser with a big, ugly butt. He turns around and looks at me questioningly. I take over.

What never happens will happen today. This is the decisive breakaway. I'll pass Despuech like a piece of fluff, shake off Sauveplane like a tattered washcloth on the first climb, for the final hundred kilometers I'll solo out in front, my victory will be talked about for years to come.

I feel the burning pain that forms the bridge between attack and rhythm. I must be crazy! If they leave me alone, I'll be a prisoner to my own enthusiasm. Let Krabbé go on doggy-paddling. All they have to do is stay two hundred meters behind me until I ride myself into the ground, or humiliate myself by falling back.

Sauveplane takes over again, I look around. The bunch is coming back, Barthélemy's thick lenses out in front, a few slots behind him the green jersey of Reilhan. Such an honor. Sauveplane looks around accusingly and stops moving his legs.

Barthélemy flies past me right away, followed by a rushing ribbon of ten, twenty riders. I yank myself back into motion and hop a wheel, behind me a mild curse from the guy I've blocked. Slowing, speeding up, someone else must have attacked, I fly along, pass Barthélemy, who pops up off the saddle for new speed. In front of us suddenly, another glimpse of Despuech. Poor bastard.

Again someone jumps and the ribbon accelerates, then the pack grows quiet. The hunt for the fresh summer breeze is over. Now that I have time to think again, it occurs to me that there was nothing crazy about my attacking like that. How could I have forgotten? I always do that in the first few kilometers, just to get the blood flowing.

Riders sit up, tidy their breathing. The pace slows further. Despuech has disappeared around the bends again. Was he hoping we'd catch up with him?

Slowly but powerfully, like an old black taxi, Sauveplane pulls away from the peloton once more. He glances around, sails to the left side of the road, shoots past an oncoming car and is gone, followed a bit later by a boy in a light-blue jersey from Cycles Goff. He looks vaguely familiar.

We'll be seeing Sauveplane again, but is it a good idea to let Cycles Goff go like that? I don't have any *domestiques* to control the course, not like Barthélemy. My club is weak. I have only my secret pact with Teissonnière, but Teissonnière is a contender himself, he'd rather save his strength.

It's too early. Henri Pélissier once said: 'Always attack as late as you can, but before the others do.'

In fact, there's no need for me to worry. In this race there are

15

two strong rival clubs: Nîmes and Alès. Nîmes has Reilhan, Boutonnet, Guillaumet; Alès has Barthélemy and Kléber. If they don't take the bait, then so be it. They want to win too, and the heaviest burden rests with the strong. Sauveplane and Despuech are both lesser riders from Alès; if Reilhan is worried, he and his club will simply have to close the gap.

The calm in the peloton continues. Up ahead I see Cycles Goff and Sauveplane taking turns at the pull, a few minutes later they disappear from sight as well. Soon they'll be with Despuech. A car with wheels on the roof passes the peloton, beeping its horn. 'Cycles Goff' is painted on the side. The car from Alès sticks with Barthélemy.

Along the road a little boy points to his watch and shouts something. I make out the word 'seconds'.

Kilometer 10. The Tour de Mont Aigoual has three lead riders, tolerated by the pack. We pass two villages, receive applause in both.

As a journalist, I only once followed a major race: Paris–Roubaix, 1976. I found out then how right they are when they say that reporters see nothing. In my case, I didn't hear anything either: because of a mix-up, the car I shared with a few other journalists didn't even have an official shortwave radio. We had to make do with an eyewitness account from a Belgian sports announcer, who was sitting on the back of a motorcycle in the thick of the race. The wonders of technology: driving through France and listening to Radio Brussels!

The only riders I saw up close during the seven hours of

16

that race were Martinez, Talbourdet and Boulas: three Frenchmen. They escaped after the first kilometer, and one hour later they had a ten-minute lead. With the spring breeze at their backs they were doing a little under fifty kilometers an hour, fast for just three riders. Their team managers with the spare parts simply stayed back with their aces in the bunch; if one of the three had come down with a puncture, he would have had to sit out his entire lead along the road. That's what I was hoping would happen, so I could wait with the luckless sod, jot down his misery and tell him that I was a racer too.

Everywhere people stood clapping and screaming for Martinez, Talbourdet and Boulas. '*Vas-y, Poupou!*' That was exactly it: they had wanted and were allowed to escape precisely because they didn't stand a chance.

I have an aversion to the expression 'allowed to escape', because it usually comes from people who have no notion of the tremendous power needed for that 'being allowed to', but it's a fact: no trio of riders could ever escape and stay away from an unwilling peloton in the first kilometers of a flat race. Forget about Koblet.

Martinez, Talbourdet and Boulas rode for hours through human hedgerows in the festive north of France, and everywhere they received a hero's welcome — precisely because they weren't heroes.

Not one of the three won Paris–Roubaix.

Kilometer 15. Suddenly, a tandem jump by Boutonnet and an unfamiliar rider in a Molteni jersey. They must have been plotting that one. 'Ho hey, ho hey' goes the peloton, but no one does a thing about it. The pace actually seems to drop. This is serious; Nîmes now has a man out in front as well, and Boutonnet is one of the better riders. I see him gliding away from me with huge sweeps of the pedals. Downstream through the canyon in his twelve.

I move to the front, pick up the pace a little. If a few of the fellows would help out now, we'd have the whole break back just like that. Ha, here's Lebusque again. But once I've traded off with him a few times, I notice that we're the only ones willing to take our pull. I look back, find Guillaumet sitting on my wheel. I raise my eyebrows. He raises his eyebrows too, and shrugs. Nîmes.

What am I supposed to do? The pack is a prison. I stop pedaling, Guillaumet stops pedaling, Lebusque waits in vain for relief and looks at me like he wants to throw me out of a restaurant. The bunch thickens. Brakes cackle against rims. I turn around. 'Goddamn it, are you racers or do we get off right here!' Nobody gets off. I squeeze my brakes and drop back to the middle of the pack.

Sanchez breaks away, the peloton is treading water. There's no way out of this. Mustn't lose my patience. Teissonnière jumps too. That's better. To my surprise, everyone lets him go. In the blink of an eye, he and Sanchez are up with Boutonnet and the Molteni man.

Like me, Teissonnière is a lone wolf in the peloton. We help each other a little. I don't chase him and he doesn't chase me. We say. If we reach the finale together, I'll open slots for him, and if that doesn't work he'll pull the sprint for me. No one's found out yet, I think, which makes our alliance that much more effective.

But a victory for Teissonnière is not a victory for me – and if he wins, no one will know that I've won a little too. And meanwhile the four disappear around bends, on their way to the front. Team cars with spare parts pass the peloton. A strong lead group of seven is coming together.

Mustn't lose patience.

Shouting. It's Lebusque. He gestures to me, I act like I don't see him. I know what's going to happen. He moves to the front, picks up the pace, looks back mopingly, sees that no one's coming to help, then tucks down over his bars. A few times he drops back a little, but as soon as he's off point it seems like he remembers something and moves back up. Occasionally he shouts, but no one helps. Don't look at me. Bicycle racing is a sport of patience. 'Racing is licking your opponent's plate clean before starting on your own.' Hennie Kuiper said that. Lebusque will stay out in front for kilometers. Where would we be without Lebusque?

Lebusque doesn't know what racing is.

Kilometer 15–25. Bicycle racing is boring, all of a sudden I remember thinking that last time too. So why do I do it? Why are you climbing that mountain? Because it's there, says the alpinist.

We've left the Jonte; at a town where people clapped for us we turned right, and now we're riding along the Tarn, a bigger river, with kayaks in the water. The gorge is wider, the walls higher. The travel books call the Gorges du Tarn the most beautiful canyon in Europe.

One plus two plus two plus two is seven. That's right, seven. Out in front of us, a lead group of seven must have formed by now: Teissonnière, Despuech, Sanchez, the rider from Cycles Goff, Sauveplane, Boutonnet, and I can't think of the seventh. Still, it's a nice idea: as far as I know, Teissonnière is the strongest of that group.

Every once in a while someone along the road lets us know how far behind we are. A man shouts: 'Faster!' Probably thinks bicycle racing is about going fast.

I ride beside Barthélemy for a bit. He stares straight ahead. He comes out of the saddle to stretch his legs, then sits again. I look over at him, but he acts like he doesn't see me. I know what he's thinking; of all the favorites, he's the worst climber. The wall we have to go up is waiting for us across the river — a real bastard of a climb.

Everywhere I come, the lead riders have been there, two, three, four minutes before me; it's like being handed a newspaper with the front page torn off. No worse way to follow a road race than to be in it.

My sporting career: 1973
I was sitting in a café in Anduze, reading the *Midi Libre*. The regional pages announced a bicycle race that would start and finish in Anduze itself. Suddenly I sensed that it was now or never. I'd been cycling every day for the last few months and

keeping track of my times, but racing was something I only dreamed of.

The organizer's name was Stéphan. I went looking for him and asked whether I could join the race. I also asked whether he was *the* Stéphan, the Stéphan who had ridden in the Tour de France. He was. He'd even finished one: in 1954, riding for Southeast France, he'd come in sixty-sixth. Now he was the owner of a vineyard outside Anduze and chairman of the local road-racing club, which he signed me up for right away, and he also organized regional amateur races. He seemed amused to meet someone who would be riding his first race at the age of twenty-nine, and I had him tell me about the Tour.

'So it's going to be an international race on Sunday,' Stéphan said. He sent me to the doctor for a health certificate, and arranged my starting permit.

I was a racer!

Race 1, on March 11, 1973: a time trial over thirty-three kilometers. The course included a climb; at least, I thought it was a climb. But while I was moving uphill in my lightest gear, sweat pouring from the corners of my eyes, looking up again and again to see whether the end might be coming around the curves, a rider went tearing past me. Later I heard that he'd started six minutes after me. He wore thick glasses. He stood on the pedals, held his bars low, and he was going at least twice as fast as I was. Behind him came a tiny car full of family members, who didn't even look at me. The way they slid past, staring straight ahead, underscored that rider's power.

At the top, where I was finally allowed to begin the fourteen-kilometer return to Anduze, I saw him again. Far out in front of me in the rolling landscape, he was knocking back one hundred-meter marker after the other, that tiny car bouncing along behind. I thought: 'I'm still riding my very first race.'

Back in Anduze I went up to that rider. His name was Barthélemy, and he had won, he still had the bouquet in his hand. I had come in number forty-one in a field of forty-nine. Of course number forty-one isn't supposed to just start talking to number one, but being exotic made up for a great deal. Barthélemy offered me a slug from his bottle of Evian. In one gulp I tossed down 3600000000000000000000000 water molecules, thousands of which are in my body even now. I asked if he remembered passing me. He did, which surprised me greatly. He even knew where.

'What were you climbing on there?' I asked.

'Fifty-three sixteen.'

'Gee,' I said.

For the rest of that day, during which I thought dozens of times: 'This is still the day that I rode my very first race,' I reflected on how the eight riders who'd come in after me were real racers too, people who trained a lot. In the weeks to come, as I unofficially wormed my way up in the classification of that time trial and went on to ride my second, third and following races, I discovered that this Barthélemy was the best rider in the region. He won all the time, and was particularly invincible in the sprint. Every rider has a rider he dreams about. I dreamed of one day being as good as Barthélemy.

Kilometer 25–30. A little boy with a rear-view mirror and fluttering ribbons on his handlebars cycles along beside us and yells: 'You guys aren't going fast at all! You're all a bunch of assholes!' Guillaumet rides over to him, grabs the back of his saddle, brakes and comes back a little later, boyless.

Laughter.

But the laughter dies down, and the talking does too. 'It's weird that you already know it but your body doesn't,' someone said to me once, half an hour before I climbed Mont Ventoux.

Every new kilometer stone is closer to Les Vignes, and at Les Vignes we'll cross the Tarn: there begins the climb to the Causse Méjean, the high plateau. The wall we have to go up, a hard steel blue from here, waits calmly across the river. Riders start glancing to the right more often, then straight ahead, then to the right again, at that wall.

Kilometer 30–31. The last kilometer before the bridge. I look to the right.

Suddenly I see our lead riders.

That must be them! A few dots crawling along, surprisingly high already, with cars behind. A slight feeling of impropriety: like accidentally catching a glimpse of a woman in the nude, a woman I'm in love with but have never laid hands on. I look at my watch.

There's the bridge. A few slots ahead of me, Kléber pulls his water bottle from its holder and stuffs it in his back pocket.

○

Kilometer 31. A sign: LES VIGNES. At the crossing by the bridge is a gendarme, pointing to the right. Right turn, over the bridge. I buckle down and shift to my inside ring, other chains rattling around me. Anyone still on his outside ring when the hill starts is in for trouble. They'll have to shift on the climb: when you do that, the chain clutches at thin air for a second with incredible force, in the worst of cases popping across the sprocket like a machine gun and throwing you off balance. Photograph of rider with bicycle, lying in gravel: 'Rider Kr. learning the technique of the uphill shift.'

To the right. A five-kilometer climb to the Causse Méjean. I've dropped back a little; I'm in the middle of the peloton.

Mayhem. A rider shifts, misses his gear, almost somersaults over his bars, curses. Twenty riders in front of me now, a whole road full. I pick out Lebusque, a hang-glider among starlings.

The worst gaps arise during climbs. I have to work my way up to the front. Weaving back and forth, I search for openings. Panic that they're going to leave me behind, I still can't feel my pedals. I tap someone's back wheel, I swerve, someone else pushes off of me, I end up on the shoulder, no puncture.

24

Whoosh, whoosh. Two riders gone. With a few simple strokes they go cycling out of my race. Reilhan and Guillaumet. The true men of respect here – between races I just kid myself.

And in a flash they're really gone for good. Making a jump uphill is highly effective, but also the toughest thing there is. Bahamontes, Fuente, could do it twenty times in a row, like buck rabbits. All run-of-the-mill climbers warn each other about guys like that. Don't go after them. You go after them anyway? They'll just go again, they'll yo-yo you to death.

Meanwhile, however, I'll end up the anonymous tenth. All I can do is accept it. I can only do what I'm doing and keep doing that.

I've ended up at the front of our half-jump-drained peloton. Third position. That's where I'm staying; the two guys in front of me are going fast enough. After a while it dawns on me who they are: Lebusque and Kléber, side by side. Lebusque is standing on his pedals in an enormous gear, but going smoothly. Kléber is sitting. Behind me and to one side, pumping, groaning, but, surprisingly enough, it's Barthélemy.

Gradually I find a cadence. Climbing is a rhythm, a trance; you have to rock your organs' protests back to sleep.

The road is empty and narrow. Everything here has to do with stone. Stones on the road, overhanging rocks. Everywhere the bleached elephant gray of stone. Along the road poppies and hundred-meter markers. Lots of poppies and few hundred-meter markers. A hairpin turn, every once in a while a view below. It's all there: height, clear water, rugged crags. 'The riders had little opportunity to admire the breathtaking landscape.'

A hundred-meter marker.

I'm riding forty-three eighteen. Too high. I'll have to go to the nineteen, but if I put it off until I get to that stone marker the race is mine. Interview with Lucien Van Impe's mechanic, after a major mountain stage: 'His twenty-two was still clean as a whistle.' Meaning: he rode easily today, he didn't need that painkiller.

I shift down. Forty-three nineteen: the gear of champions. How the hell do I keep talking myself into racing?

Kilometer 32–34. Seven plus two is nine. Still, I'm not climbing badly, that amazes me every time. It hurts, but it's also sort of nice. Heavy labor you can handle, carrying a pile of pouffes up to your girlfriend's new apartment.

Keep the steer steady, going slow here. The way I see it, your handlebars move forward and you just have to make sure you don't let go. You need strong arms for that. I view my wrists, stretched out in front of me to the bars, straight as ramrods. They've become so tanned, almost black in the wrinkles. The little hairs lie next to each other in wet rows, pointing away from me. I find my wrists incredibly beautiful.

I climb.

What I can do, no animal can: be the other and admire myself. I hear nothing and see nothing, but I sense that, behind me, one rider after the other is being dropped. I once

26

interviewed an Olympic rower, Jan Wienese. Rowers practice their sport backwards. I asked Wienese whether he was ever afraid, during training sessions for example, of running into something. 'No, we have radar for that,' he said.

They may have been dropped by the dozen, but I sprinkle my back with the glances of riders behind me. Cool and collected, that Krabbé. Did you see him? Pow-er.

Do my eyes deceive me, or are we gaining a little on Reilhan and Guillaumet?

Race 44, August 15, 1973. There goes the thirty-year-old Dutch rider Kr. through the woods, as last of a lead group of sixteen. The road climbs a little, they're taking the first slopes of the Col du Mercou, one of the silliest cols in all the Cévennes.

Slightly perplexed, I noticed that the others were going faster than I was. Perplexed, because I wasn't straining or anything, my legs didn't even hurt, at least not the kind of hurt that sticks to paper these many years later. I just couldn't go any faster.

The group was slowly sliding away from me. How sad. There went race number forty-four, sailing out of my life for ever.

I had an excuse, though: it was my first real mountain race, and this was already the second col. On the first one I'd had no trouble keeping up, I'd almost had to laugh with pleasure, seeing the row of dancing backs out in front of me, something I'd only seen till then on TV or in films. It even occurred to me to sprint for the premium at the summit, a plan I quickly forgot when riders various and sundry began cycling past me. I noted the order in which I crossed the line: eleventh. Out of sixty-one! Not too shabby! Unfortunately, I took a slide on the second curve of the descent. My first fall during a race! By the time I'd scrambled to my feet and continued down, the main bunch was gone from sight.

One other rider passed me and, after a grim chase that lasted three-quarters of an hour, we caught up with the lead riders, partly because they were taking it easy before that next col. Which followed immediately on the heels of our successful hunt.

And off they rode, the whole colorful troupe. Ten meters, twelve meters, twelve-point-zero-one meters.

Forty meters.

'Why'd you let them go?'

'I couldn't do it.'

'Just one more kick, couldn't you have managed that?'

'Yeah, God, one kick, yeah.'

'So why didn't you?'

'I couldn't.'

I didn't see them any more. I was a dropped rider, I was a thirty-year-old Dutchman in a red jersey trying to cycle up a hill. Team cars passed me, then the forest was quiet again.

I rode the next fifty kilometers on my own, until a group of stragglers caught up with me. With them I finished the final fifty, feeling like I was dragging my soul on a string. I came in third in our sprint, eighteenth in total. I asked all the riders who'd been in the break about how the rest of the race had gone, and how much earlier they'd come in. Their estimates varied from seven to twenty-five minutes.

Storybook creatures.

There we have Gerrie Knetemann. These days he lives in Brabant, but it's December 4, 1977, and he's back in Amsterdam for a few days' vacation, out for a light training run with our group. I cycle beside him, and the conversation turns to climbing.

'You guys need to suffer more, get dirtier; you should arrive at the top in a casket, that's what we pay you for,' I say.

'No,' Knetemann says, 'you guys need to describe it more compellingly.'

He can't explain to me, no more than he's ever been able to in newspaper interviews, why he's such a good climber, but not on the highest cols. I try to draw him out about the horror of the moment he gets dropped, the moment he sees the others riding away from him. Doesn't it make him want to weep in pain and sorrow?

'No,' Knetemann says. 'It's too bad, sure, but at a certain point you just can't do it. And when you can't do it any more, you get dropped. Too bad. Nothing to make a fuss about.'

Kilometer 34–36. Two more kilometers to climb. Muggy. My brains are getting ready to squish out of my ears like gravy rolls. Climbing, on the wheel of Kléber in his long, low sit. Lebusque stands, and sometimes I have to get off the saddle too. We crawl up along the abyss, above the blue Tarn.

We're also crawling up to Reilhan and Guillaumet. The gap is easily a hundred meters, but I can tell now that we're going to make it. Hairpin turn. The Tarn rolls over to lie on my left.

Forty-three nineteen. How about forty-three twenty? No, on the first climb you can push things a little.

Barthélemy's clunky movements have become even clunkier. On the saddle, off the saddle, shift, drink, hands on the brakes, hands on the bars. He's biting the bullet, those glasses of his weigh ten kilos.

Suddenly he drops back. He vacates the spot beside me, he falls irrevocably from our midst. He hung in there for a long time today. How many of us are there now? When we started the climb, there were forty-six. Six or seven? I'm afraid to look back, it would break my rhythm.

Lebusque, Kléber, out in front. During our practice ride, Kléber had already dropped me long before this. He's the best climber here today, he's little and skinny. On weekdays he works at the exchange window of a bank in Alès. If you saw him there, you'd never think he's a bicycle racer, and sometimes it's like that when he races too. In the criteriums, that scrambling in the streets, he always quits within fifteen minutes. Then he just stands there at the point where he climbed off, leaning against his bike with a slow smile, watching the others fight it out. He never roots for anyone.

There's always something to blame. Evil powers are

constantly thwarting him. His stomach was acting up. His leg hurt so bad. His tire was soft. His chain slipped. Something broke.

He doesn't mind when I insult him. He takes a lot from me, because we're friends.

'Stani, you never really push things. I think you're a pansy. What kind of a rider are you?' He looks at me and says that I could very well be right.

'I'm absolutely right.'

'Yes, absolutely.' As from today, he's going to change the way he races.

'I don't believe it for a minute.'

But in the long, tough road races, when there are mountains to fight instead of a whirlwind of riders, Kléber shines. Because he never attacks, and because there's always someone who can stick with him and beat him in the sprint, he's never won a race. He has no panache, no brio, no *courage*.

He lives to ride.

We're gaining on three men in front of us. Three? While I'm trying to figure that one out, I see that the third rider is already dropping behind Reilhan and Guillaumet. Must be Despuech. After a full tenth of a second, though, I see that it isn't Despuech, it's someone three times his size: Sauveplane. He's standing on the pedals, jerking his head back and forth in a parody of strength. Still, he's one of the lead riders, the first one back in my sights.

Sauveplane has squandered his strength. He can't stick

with Reilhan and Guillaumet, of course, and he won't be able to stick with us. He's going to get dropped like a kilometer stone.

As I pass him, I look over. Earnest. All the pious earnestness of the vanquished sportsman. He doesn't stand a chance, but he's making the best of it!

And the crowd falls for it every time! How often have I seen people clapping and cheering for a rider who, having been lapped six times, pushes on bravely? It's an insulting brand of applause – for where does a winning rider get the right to revel in applause if the crowd isn't obliged to hiss at him when he fails?

A hard stretch of hill. I'm not going to shift down, though, I come up off the saddle, I'm pushing it. One more kilometer to climb. It's so incredibly pitiful that I ever wanted to do this, but now I'm stuck with it.

Major developments: in front of me, Guillaumet is dropping back, Reilhan is continuing on his own. Hang tight. I'm between the back wheels of Kléber and Lebusque. My legs feel black. Guillaumet's falling apart completely now, he's treading water; we ride past him. I can tell he won't be able to tough this one out, he's finished. Now I remember: Guillaumet should never have been here in the first place, Guillaumet is incapable of sweating blood, he only shows class in the little spins around the village.

We're gaining on Reilhan, Kléber bridges the final gap, our approach is silent, like a spaceship ready for docking.

We're there. Reilhan fades back till he's on Kléber's back wheel.

Cadence. Half a kilometer to go. Before me my beautiful wrists, a hundred kilometers of race, and far, far away, a six-man break. How many of us are still here? Don't look around. How fast are we going, anyway? I should count the turns of the pedal, by the minute, figure out my gearing. How much is forty-three divided by nineteen?

A blank. I *become* the number forty-three and stick out the leg of my four to pull the nineteen over to me, but nothing happens, we remain lying chastely side by side.

Kléber, Lebusque and, beside me, Reilhan.

When I withdrew to Anduze in 1973 for my first period of cyclo-literary hermitry, I believed that, while cycling, I would come up with thoughts and ideas for the stories I'd be writing the rest of the time. Fat chance. The rest of my time I spent jotting in my cycling logbook and keeping statistics on my distances and times, and while cycling I thought of nothing at all.

On a bike your consciousness is small. The harder you work, the smaller it gets. Every thought that arises is immediately and utterly true, every unexpected event is something you'd known all along but had only forgotten for a moment. A pounding riff from a song, a bit of long division that starts over and over, a magnified anger at someone, is enough to fill your thoughts.

During the race, what goes round in the rider's mind is a

monolithic ball bearing, so smooth, so uniform, that you can't even see it spin. Its almost perfect lack of surface structure ensures that it strikes nothing that might end up in the white circulation of thought. Almost nothing, that is – sometimes a microscopic flaw still manages to strike a chord. From race number 203 (evening criterium at Groot Ammers, May 30, 1975) I remember the sound *brrr-ink*, pronounced as two syllables, that popped into my mind every time at the same street corner, twenty, thirty, sixty laps long, that I ruminated over, the way tongue and teeth can play with a half-forgotten wad of gum a feature film long, until I was back at that corner and *brrr-ink* was refreshed in its original form.

Why not some other corner? Why *brrr-ink*? We know little of the workings of the human mind, as a mass murderer's lawyer once told the courtroom.

I once gave myself the assignment of inventing a completely random word. Completely random, is that possible? And all of a sudden, there it was: Battoowoo Greekgreek.

Battoowoo Greekgreek. Is that a name? I don't know anyone who answers to that. No one will ever be able to tell me where Battoowoo Greekgreek came from. A few million years of evolution haven't resulted in brains that can understand themselves. Why is there, somewhere along a training route near Amsterdam, an elm that reminds me of the chess grandmaster Jan Hein Donner? Every time I see that elm I think 'Donner', and then I see him before me ten meters tall.

34

That kind of thing.

No, then give me chess! As soon as you start playing, the smooth monolithic bearing is replaced, as in a modern typewriter, by a ball covered with ridges, angles, bumps, protuberances. That ball spins around like mad, indiscriminately knocking all kinds of things into your consciousness. Soup that was too cold, seven years ago now; an old game lost to an up-and-coming youth champion with a completely different opening, but with exactly the same brand of chewy caramels beside the board; a botched perpetual-motion machine you saw somewhere. Six new things every minute, to say nothing of the conversations with other players during the game that sometimes actually have subjects.

In bicycle racing, that's all different. Which is why I don't believe the rider who, during a training session in the dunes between Noordwijk and Zandvoort, told me how he had seduced a woman during a criterium. She was standing behind a crush barrier when he discovered her, or she him. (If *she'd* told me, I would have believed her.) Every hundred seconds he came barreling past, and so their love blossomed as prettily as a flower in one of those time-lapse films. Ten laps long they smiled at each other, for another ten laps she winked, they began running their tongues over their lips, and by the time the race was approaching its decisive phase their gestures had become downright salacious. He said so, but I don't believe him, because he's a very good racer.

It's impossible. That he went to bed with someone from

35

the crowd after a race, OK. But he needs to come up with a different story.

Kilometer 36. Something else that spins: Kléber's legs. With every revolution I see the power flowing down his legs and into his pedals. Kléber and Lebusque out in front. For a moment there it occurred to me to go up front and pull the lead a little, but I kept myself in check. I may not take from Kléber what he values so highly: the right to imagine the admiration in my eyes.

The climb is over. Or is it? I'm not sure any more. The road is moving away from the gorge now, into the highlands. Occasionally there's a view out over clear fields, past bushy little trees. We all shift, almost at the same moment.

It's colder here.

This isn't a climb any more, this is a *faux plat*.

✿

Kilometer 37. Causse Méjean. Wind. Visibility out ahead, two minutes: not a thing. I straighten up and close my jersey. I look back: nothing either.

Jesus Pleaseus.

Emptiness, our team cars, then more emptiness. The visibility back there is at least two minutes as well. We've ditched them all! Man for man, all they could do was give up, sick with fatigue, pained to have to let us go, and their final thought was: 'Damn, that Krabbé cruises along like it's nothing.'

I have destroyed them.

When, at the end of his career, they asked Rudi Altig about his greatest race, he didn't mention his world road championship of 1966 or his victory in the Spanish Vuelta in 1962, his yellow jerseys in the Tour de France or his numerous pursuit championships. He spoke of the Trofeo Baracchi of 1962.

He'd won that one too, but that wasn't why he chose it. What Altig had always loved about that race (a time trial for two man teams) was that he had ridden his brace-mate, Anquetil, right into the ground; during the last forty of the 111 kilometers, Anquetil hadn't even been able to take his pull at the front.

Wonderful photos, those: Altig, that marble German, turning around on his bike and bellowing at the cramped, fatigue-green Monsieur Chrono. Photos of Altig pushing Anquetil, pulling him, screaming him on, chastising him with his support.

When they rode into the stadium, Anquetil was so drained that he didn't make the curve, and simply plopped over like a book on a bookshelf. There was blood coming from a cut on his head, he couldn't go on, he gave up. Lucky for him the clock had stopped when the riders entered the stadium: that last lap was only for the show, he'd won anyway.

Photos of Anquetil being lifted from the ground, a trickle

of blood running down his cheek, eyes filled with dread, photos of him being carried away between two strong men – not to the victor's scaffold, but to the catacombs, like an old man being pulled from the wreckage of a hurricane.

Kilometer 37–44. Barthélemy dumped, Petit dumped, Wolniak dumped, Quincy, Sauveplane, Lange dumped, you name it! Guillaumet dumped! Four strong men are all that's left: Kléber, Lebusque, Reilhan and me.

'Ride, guys, we've blown a gap!' I scream.

We've blown a gap all right, but exactly how far behind the leaders are we? Completely forgot to look at my watch just now. Four minutes? Five? How did Despuech keep from getting ditched on that climb?

We all pull the lead at regular intervals. The road is straight and leads upward. *Faux plats* of one-half, then one percent, you can never find a rhythm, the wind blows. Here and there a little side road paved with broken stone, leading to something that should have been blown away long ago.

The wind is crossing at our backs, we're going fast. I hope the pace is high enough to keep Barthélemy from coming back: Barthélemy can't climb, but he can fight. I've clamped on to Reilhan's wheel to make sure he takes his turns out front. And that, of course, is exactly what he doesn't do, he just pretends to. Whenever he takes over he gives five real kicks, and then simulates speed.

This kid is such an asshole, the whole idea of racing is to squander energy, isn't it? Kléber is working, I'm working, Lebusque is working for three, so why shouldn't Reilhan?

But trying to keep him up front any longer will only cost us our tempo.

'Goddamn it, Reilhan, if you're tired, lie down and take a nap!' I shout. He leaves the lead to me and rolls back to the tail of the group. It didn't sink in. On his face the smile that always stays the same, uphill and down again, the smile of the golden boy.

Should I give him some more hell?

It's too early in the race to pick a fight. And in fact, with his teammate Boutonnet up there in the lead group, I should be happy with every meter Reilhan pulls.

Besides, maybe Reilhan really loves to squander energy; maybe it's just that his father – a fat little man with a grim marmot-face who follows him everywhere – won't let him.

His father is supposed to have been a pro at one time, but I've never heard of him. He never rode in the Tour, that's for sure. His wife sits in the passenger seat, together they trail along behind Reilhan in every race he rides.

Long, straight road.

My sporting career: 1972
I'd bought myself a racing bike. For the first six months it leaned against a bookcase. On July 20, 1972, I decided to take it out for a spin, even though I knew I was starting something that might get me in over my head. It was a hot day, and when I came home I had to hold my wrists under the cold tap for fifteen minutes.

Fun was different, but now I was cycling every day.

Always the same route, just under forty kilometers, so I could compare my times. At first I broke my own record by minutes at a shot, then I'd remain hanging against a ceiling for weeks, then suddenly pop through to a next level and nibble seconds off that, until I gradually started wondering whether I was getting good.

I needed to calculate my average speed. My watch was working, so the problem facing me was: how does a private citizen measure a distance?

Oskar Egg's solution seemed hardly suitable. Egg had been holder of the World Hour Record for almost twenty years when, in 1933, news came that a Dutchman, Jan van Hout, had broken it. There's a standard line for dethroned record-holders: 'It was about time; I'm pleased for the kid.' Egg immediately traveled to Roermond, where the new record had been set, crawled around the track with a yard-stick and announced that it was shorter than it was supposed to be. Van Hout hadn't broken the record, he'd shrunken it! That's where the anecdote ends, because four days later the record was broken again by a Frenchman, this time in a fashion that defied Egg's yardstick.

I studied the map (lay a string along the roads, multiply by scale), I drove the route in my car, in a friend's car, I mounted an odometer on my bike, but every measurement produced a different result; the object to be measured only proved the lameness of my methods.

Then it came to me in a flash. I would adopt the Egg Method anyway, but then using the yardstick as a means of transportation. A bicycle, after all, is a yardstick; with every turn of the pedal you travel the same distance. I selected the forty-eight nineteen, which meant that with every turn of the pedals I would cover 48 divided by 19 times 2.133 meters (the circumference of a wheel + inflated tire): 5.39 meters.

The trick was to keep riding in the same gear, to keep pedaling and to count the turns of the pedal. A first attempt failed, however, when I lost count somewhere around three thousand.

The next time I took a little sack of eighty matchsticks with me. After every hundred turns of the pedal, I threw away one match. By counting the leftover matches when I got home, subtracting that number from eighty, multiplying that by one hundred, adding the number of turns at the end that hadn't produced a thrown-away match and multiplying all that by 5.39, I had the exact length of my training route in meters.

The length of my route was 37,855.66 meters.

Kilometer 44. A sign: COL DE RIEISSE, altitude 920 m.

Every time I take a pull up front, I feel it: I'm strong today. So what if I attacked right here?

Then my chances would be reduced.

Correct.

I stopped doing everything else, I trained harder and harder, my body began achieving things I'd no longer thought possible. I was touched by its loyalty. I had neglected it for so long, but there were no hard feelings, it seemed only pleased to have me call on it again. I raced with Stéphan in Anduze, I applied for a permit in Holland – full of disbelief, I worked my way up in those races through the hierarchy of being dropped, of sticking with the bunch, of taking part in a break, taking part in *the* break, of placing, of winning.

And every year I went back to Anduze to see whether my dream was going to come true. I rode well in those wonderful, killing races through the Cévennes. I came in seventh, fifth, second a few times, I won. I won more often. When all around me were cracking, I was at my best. I cracked too, but I still attacked and won. 'A paragon of willpower, the scourge of the peloton,' *Midi Libre* wrote. 'You know, you could have been a good average pro if you'd started when you were sixteen,' Stéphan said.

Even though I stole the occasional victory from him, even though we attacked each other so often that everything went black, even though I ditched him on the *cols*, Barthélemy liked me. He remembered the moment he'd passed me in Race 1 like it was yesterday. 'You sure had a fat ass back then.'

Finally, I started winning as often as he did. And when a new rider, Reilhan, rose up and began stealing even more of his victories, Barthélemy came to me one day and said: 'You know what, Krabbé? We have to work together. I don't go after you, you don't go after me. OK?'

Kilometer 44–55. It doesn't happen very often: suddenly there's a sign along the road showing that you've just climbed a col. COL DE RIEISSE, good. Now come the *faux plats* going down, making it even harder to find a rhythm; that's all there is to it.

Desolation, abandoned farms. From what I've read, it can get down to minus twenty-five here in the winter. We pass a ghost town – there are lots of them around here. Houses, no people. The people have vanished, lured by the horrors of the big city, and the ones who are still around go out and paint signs: TOURISTS, TAKE A HIKE.

A silent plane passes over us. They do a lot of skydiving around here. Reilhan, I'm so sick of you.

Seventeen kilometers of high plateau to go.

Been riding for an hour and a half, the same faces all around. We turn right, up a broad road that runs past the blustery tourist attractions of the high plateau. Caverns, and spots where one finds oneself precisely one kilometer above sea level. The first signs showing the distance back to Meyrueis. We won't catch sight of the lead riders before then. In any case, we won't have to sprint for the premiums at Meyrueis. Wind in the face now.

The strange feeling steals over me that we *are* the lead riders. I eat a fig.

A huge smack on my left arm. A stone, but the stone won't go away, it's a bee. A gigantic bee that's drilled its stinger into my arm. If it had eyes, they'd be big enough to stare me in the face. It's just sitting there now, riding along in the Tour de Mont Aigoual. Is it true that bees die after the first sting?

A dull ache burns its way up my arm: the venom. By

43

reflex, I slap the bee with my other hand and it flies off. I see the stinger in my skin. I pull it out.

Reilhan: 'Did that bee get you?' Genuine concern, you'd think.

A couple of hundred years of velvet cushions have rendered our reflexes obsolete, but haven't wiped them out. I automatically pinch my left arm as hard as I can; a brown fluid comes out of the sting, the little puddle dries up, the pain is gone, I forget it.

A village: Aumières.

My sporting career: 1970
Driving through southern Norway, I saw two skydivers floating down from heaven under flowery tarps. I pulled over and watched. I figured out where they must have come down, drove there, and asked a man in a leather suit standing beside a plane whether I could make a jump too. One hour later I had signed up for a skydiving course, and three days later I jumped. Then I continued north.

That summer I returned to the customs of my youth. In Copenhagen I found a Dutch paper with a list of all the participants in the Tour de France. On a whim I also bought a sheet of construction paper, a notepad, a pair of scissors, magic markers and a pair of dice. I cut out little rectangles and put the names of all the Tour riders on them; then used the construction paper to make a board on which I played the stages of the Tour. If the stage was 224 kilometers long, I had the riders cover 224 spaces. I figured out all the classifications, and the rider who held the yellow jersey received a new, yellow square of paper. One of the pieces of paper had the name Krabbé on it.

What had never happened before happened now. In Oslo I captured the yellow jersey. At Stavanger I lost it again to the Italian Zilioli, but I regained it at Narvik, and a few thousand kilometers further, in Helsinki, I still held it. I stayed there for a week. I rented a room in a student apartment house, with a view of a wispy birch forest. Every day, before descending into the hum of downtown, I would spend five or six hours playing two stages. When I came back in the evening I would play another one. I lost the yellow jersey, I sank far in the ranks.

Every once in a while, accompanied by the sound of snapping birch limbs, people in jogging suits would appear in the woods. The sun shone, I could hear them panting, and I would watch until they disappeared from sight. Then I went on with the Tour de France.

Finns have always been good long-distance runners.

Kilometer 55–59. In the distance a sea of motionless, faint-blue waves, one hiding the other: the hills. Beyond that must be Mont Aigoual. Dark-gray hoses hanging from the sky, as if the mountain has to be refueled. Aqua, the watery mountain. Cold wind. I've looked around a few times, seen nothing.

Psss. The familiar rattle, but my rims keep rolling along a tire's breadth above the ground. Nothing hisses quite so sweetly as a rival's puncture. It's Lebusque, which makes it less sweet. A quick glance around, I see him dropping back, rattling to a stop on his rim.

We've lost a rider who's strong, who's pleased to do his work, and who cannot sprint.

Kilometer 59–61. A sign: MEYRUEIS 8.

Shadows fly across the plateau. And then suddenly I see, far out in front of us, a tiny group of dots in a snatch of sunlight. The leaders in the Tour de Mont Aigoual. That must be the edge of the gorge; in a moment they'll be starting the descent into Meyrueis.

They pass a gas station, I glance at my watch. The next time I take over at the front, they've disappeared around the bend, into the abyss.

Since Lebusque fell behind, our pace has dropped. If I gave just one extra kick up in front, could I jack up our speed enough to make Reilhan start helping, without him noticing it? A waste of effort. The descent will be coming up any minute: that will sort out our pace by itself.

A final stretch, gradually rolling up, and we're at the gas station. Their lead: two minutes and something.

○

Kilometer 61. A hundred and fifty meters away is a big, square house. It looks like I could reach out and grab it, with its big, melancholy shutters closed tight, but between us lies a few million years of erosion. One wall of the house rises up as an extension of a chasm too deep to grasp. A rip in the earth with no conceivable bottom; the grand past of the swimming creek we came by.

Kilometer 61–67. The first kilometer downhill has a safety net of pastures, and then I find myself on the ledge along the rock. Fear of heights, multiplied by my velocity. Don't look to the side. The wind blows right through me.

I've made sure I'm out in front. It's harder to pass a rider during a descent, and the longer I keep anyone from passing me, the less the damage will be. It's not a question of *whether* I'll get dumped. Descents scare me, I'm the worst downhill rider here.

Out of the corner of my eye, a green glimpse: it's Reilhan trying to get past me; I force myself to take another kick and he drops back. A sign. It says that the speed limit here is 60 kilometers per hour My brain flashes a joke for my approval: point at that sign and waggle my finger at the others. Joke rejected.

Curves.

I'm afraid, and for good reason. Only three weeks ago, during the Dauphiné Libéré, the young up-and-coming Hinault flew out of a curve, into a ravine. Gone. At that moment the French TV audience had every reason to assume that he was lying down there with a broken back. Then he climbed up, was given another bike, rode on, won the stage and went on to win the Dauphiné Libéré. A star for ever. Hinault had gone into that ravine as a rider, but came out a *vedette*, and the entire operation had lasted no more than fifteen seconds.

Our downhill stretches are even more dangerous. For us, and even on the minor professional circuit, the roads are simply not closed to traffic. The decisions I make so hurriedly project an ineradicable dotted line in front of me, onto which cars can appear, and what then? Around every curve it may turn out that my dotted line points into the abyss, or up against a wall of rock. What also pleases me less is that I live by the grace of brake cables and tires, things truly of a lesser order than myself, though one hardly dares to say that out loud these days. Terrible accidents are out there just itching to happen. A few years ago I was still sitting safely at the chessboard; no matter how many pawns and pieces I gave away, I was safe. So why am I doing this? Because there is air, says the parachutist, because bragging about this is such a crowd-pleaser, and because I want to win Race 309.

I'm completely hopeless at this. I brake too often, and at the wrong moments. My back wheel keeps trying to skid out from under me, I wring my way clumsily through the curves. I started this sport too late. My muscles were able to fit themselves to my bike, they actually liked it: muscles are tractable and learn tricks fast. But racing downhill is a matter of nerves, and from the very start my nerves have thought: to hell with you and your bicycle racing.

You've got downhill specialists, the same way you have climbers. In our races, Reilhan is good. Barthélemy can do it, and no one can stop Lebusque. In the 1977 Tour de France, the Frenchman Rouxel was the best downhill man. During the descent of the Tourmalet that year, he bridged a gap of four and a half minutes – in terms of distance, more than five kilometers!

Rouxel says: 'I love going downhill. It's like skiing. You have to stay loose the whole time, never lock your knees – they're your shock absorbers. You have to stay down on your bike, to keep your center of gravity as low as possible. Sure, sometimes when I'm doing ninety and both wheels leave the ground, it gives me goose bumps too.'

I don't have that kind of looseness. I take the curves like a wooden puppet, afraid that my center of gravity is going to wind up in the ravine.

Race 308, June 19, 1977. There it was at last, after four years of waiting: the descent with the curve I didn't make. I'd always imagined it would be different, but now that I saw it I found it a rather silly little stretch of road.

Otherwise, though, everything was as it should have been. There was a ravine, a rock wall and a ditch. I was horrified for a moment, extremely so. Then disappointed that the race would go on without me.

After that: calm. I'd done my job. I had summoned up forces beyond my control. Those forces would have to figure out the rest for themselves. I was free. I thought: this is how I'll do it when I turn eighty. Jump out of an airplane, without a chute, and let it go.

Still, I was curious about what would happen next. I perceived how my front wheel left the road and landed in the bottom of that ditch. It seemed to be a meter and a half, two meters, deep.

My memory is full of millions of images of myself in utterly diverse situations – a number of which will be dealt

49

with elsewhere in this book. But the image of my wheel hitting the bottom of that ditch is immediately followed by one of me lying on my back in that ditch, in the position which PE instructors refer to as 'pedaling'.

I wasn't dead. I stood up. I could stand. I stepped up onto the road. I hadn't broken anything, I was not in pain. Someday I would be able to race again. I pulled my bike out of the ditch. The frame wasn't broken, the wheels were still round. The handlebars weren't bent, the tubes had not been twisted from the rims, the tires weren't flat, the chain had not jumped the ring; I'd had twice as much good luck as you'd need bad luck to get yourself killed in a fall like that.

I remounted and rode further. The whole episode had cost me fifteen seconds. After the descent, I caught up with the lead group again. I shouted: 'Bike not broken, me not broken, nothing broken!'

'Watch where you're going,' Kléber said. The bad thing was that I'd lost my bidon, and that the sections of orange in the pocket of my jersey had been juiced.

I thought: 'First Hinault, now me,' but Reilhan beat me in the sprint.

That evening Linda and I drove up so I could show her where I'd had my accident. The ditch was now thirty centimeters deep. My water bottle was still lying in it. On the way back we drank from it. No respect for monuments.

The wind is blowing tears from my eyes. I think: 'Man-oh-man.' I have to go around a car, I chicken out, but suddenly

I'm past it anyway. Another car, coming the other way. It misses me. Reilhan passes me, unstoppable, crouched, sitting way back, elegant. No way I'll be able to hold his wheel, I watch him go, watch him fly full-speed into curves I know he can't gauge. I hold my breath for him, waiting for the inert clunk of racer's body against car, but then I see him again in the loop below me.

A touring car, German plates. At the window a lady in a cheap hat looks down at me in amazement. 'The Tour of Causse Méjean was *wunderschön*, and then we saw a bicyclist by the name of Kr. go hurtling into the abyss.'

Sinning against the spirit of Rouxel I creak my way through yet another curve. A shout from Kléber. I blocked him, he passes me as soon as we're through the curve; he, the second-worst downhill man in these races. He doesn't want me getting in his way any more and pulls out in front of me, mimicking my ugly downhill style.

Suddenly, in the depths below, pointy gray roofs. Meyrueis. Rock wall to the left, abyss to the right, far too little in between. Way out in front, Reilhan in his green jersey is whipping like a madman along the outside shoulder; all it would take is one little thing interfering with his dotted line and he's dead. That his father lets him do that.

Suddenly a band of loose sand where they're fixing the road, and behind that a curve. The entire lead group must be piled up in a ditch right on the other side.

Next image: I'm through the curve. Next image: two more riders go shooting past me: Lebusque and Barthélemy. There's the sign for the limits of Meyrueis, and a hundred

meters past that the final hairpin turn. Lebusque and Barthélemy follow each other through it, light and loose on the
pedals, their seats poised a centimeter above the saddle like a
boot above a ski. The trajectory they follow has an animal
grace, lending itself to mathematical expression in a formula
of no more than four symbols – for mine you'd need a whole
scratch pad full of last-minute corrections. Before you know
it, I'm fifty meters behind.

Lebusque and Barthélemy!

But that was the last curve, another hundred thousand
years of erosion and I go flying into Meyrueis. Thank God I
can finally decide for myself how fast I want to go.

○

Kilometer 67. Curve to the right, curve to the left, watched
over by gendarmes in khaki. And the straight stretch to the
finish. I ride through a howling hedgerow.

'*Allez, Poupou!*'

'They're right up ahead!'

I try to catch a glimpse of my car. The cheering has a
rollicking overtone: we're not the first ones to come through
here.

One by one we cross the finish. The road is lined with cars
that have been shooed to one side. As we whip past them,
the drivers look at us in fright. There's the sign MEYRUEIS
again, with the red stripe through it. I can see them out in
front of me, with twenty meters between them: Kléber,
Lebusque, Barthélemy.

Kilometer 68. Here we go again. The cols here are made of air and lie upside-down in the landscape. We regroup. Six kilometers' climb to the second high plateau, the Causse Noir. I shift, move my hands up onto the bars. Pain, my legs still have to get the knack. Climbing from plateau to plateau is particularly tiring. After you get to the top, there's no descent to let you rest, and after you've been sitting still in the descent you suddenly have to give it everything you've got, without a rest.

Lebusque beside Kléber. I follow them, Barthélemy follows me, a little to one side. The first uphill part is a straightaway with a view two hundred meters ahead. Now that Reilhan is gone, I notice that I'd been hoping to catch sight of the break. I see the lenses of Barthélemy's specs, the way he looked at me when he went past. Contempt. He awards me handicaps as he sees fit, lets me horse around with my newfound powers like a farmer with a Cadillac he won in the sweepstakes.

We ride into a forest. It's dark, wet leaves, no crowd, no information. Been riding for two hours; two-and-a-half hours to go.

The road is bumpy and holey, every irregularity a drain on the rhythm I still have to find.

Forty-three nineteen. My gear lever feels like a scab on a wound. During our reconnaissance ride I was using forty-three twenty here. Now I'm sticking to the nineteen, a matter of willpower. Krabbé's twenty was still clean as a whistle. Shifting is a kind of painkiller, and therefore the

53

same as giving up. After all, if I wanted to kill my pain, why not choose the most effective method? Road-racing is all about generating pain.

Kléber still has his lightest gear in reserve, and Lebusque actually has two sprockets left. Lebusque: there's a man who *lays* his hand on the pile of bricks and *pushes* it through.

Surrounded by silence, we climb. The sweat on my wrists glistens one carat less here. Kléber rides a Mercier. It's painted on one of his tubes, and I can read it. I bicycle and can read at the same time.

Barthélemy is plugging away. Not bad of him to catch up again like that. The only one who made it. His willpower is enormous, I have to hand it to him. Only now he's going to get dropped twice, instead of only once. He has sprinters' muscles, but his talent had the bad luck to end up among the cols. Imagine Bahamontes being born in Amsterdam. He might have become a window-washer.

Kilometer 69. A kilometer marker: LANUÉJOLS 9. I remember that one. Lanuéjols is a village on Causse Noir, five kilometers beyond the end of this climb.

Four more kilometers uphill. I put my hand in my back pocket, pull out a fig. A drop of sweat on the inside of Barthélemy's glasses magnifies this action. The firm ripple of sinew with which that Krabbé lifts a fig, like it was nothing!

I chew slowly. The chews aren't linked together. The whole concept of chewing has to come up in me anew each time. I also chew on a sentence from the handbook for aspiring road racers: 'It's hard to make your jump with a mouth full of sweets.' What do you mean, make my jump?

Curves. I can never see more than twenty meters past Lebusque and Kléber's breathing. But suddenly, up to the right, there's something moving between the bushes. A rider!

Two more curves and we can see him from the back: Reilhan. One more curve and there's another rider with him: Despuech. Reilhan passes him without visible effort.

Despuech is back with us again, after more than two hours. That means the leaders can't be far. A dropped rider loses his strength and his willpower, he stands still.

Despuech looks like he's using an enormous gear, that's how slowly he's going. He's out of the saddle, he yanks at his pedals and punches them, but never will a pedal manufacturer hit on the idea of advertising that his products held up during Despuech's climb of the Causse Noir.

We pass Despuech. He sits, takes out his bidon and drinks, squirts water over his black hair. He grimaces in my direction. Water drips down his face, he opens his mouth wide, his teeth are like shards of broken glass atop a wall. In one fold of his grimace lies an apology for his body, as though that were some other person, someone we shouldn't be too hard on.

As if Despuech's collapse were some horrifying tableau that makes us pull together, we reach Reilhan within thirty seconds. Now count off. Six minus Despuech, that's five: Sanchez, Boutonnet, Teissonnière, Cycles Goff, and the guy who sticks in my mind as the one I couldn't remember last time either.

Kilometer 70. Three more kilometers to climb. I think: 'I'm climbing in a daze.'

I'd been racing around Anduze for about three years when I started running into Despuech. He came up to me and said: 'Could I borrow those Campagnolo legs of yours?' A cheerful guy of about twenty-four, always a smile, always a friendly comment. Pulling the pace line wasn't his favorite pastime, and he couldn't climb, but he did reasonably well in the little street criteriums. His specialty was the sprint for sixth place; in that he was truly invincible.

I thought: your typical flimsy sprinter.

But later Kléber told me his story. At fifteen, Despuech won every juniors' race around. The solo spurt, the two-up, sprinting against twenty other riders: whatever it took. No one could stick with him on the cols. People thought: finally, after Stéphan, we've got another really good rider here.

At sixteen, Despuech received dispensation to ride senior class. They would sometimes do races of 150 kilometers, with four or five cols. And he would win them. He won ten races when he was sixteen, twenty when was seventeen, then he burned out. At eighteen, the men whose asses he'd kicked at seventeen were leaving him in the dust. Most peculiar. He kept at it for the next year and a half, but he never got it back. He stopped. Only years later did he pick up racing again, which was when I met him. All that was left of his talent was his graceful style.

Bicycle racing is a hard sport. A rider's body has to ripen; it's also a mature sport. The average winner of the Tour de France is twenty-nine years old. You do have the occasional prodigy, but those who mean him well keep him from exhibiting it. In 1977, the nineteen-year-old Italian Saronni was one of those. He skipped over all kinds of phases and was right away one of the so-many best riders in the world. Publicity! His managers wanted him to ride the Giro d'Italia. Saronni himself thought that was a wonderful idea. But, shortly before the race, he broke his collarbone. 'The best thing that happened to Saronni in 1977,' Merckx said later, 'was that he broke his collarbone.'

Kilometer 71. Cars.

Cars and riders.

The break, I presume.

They disappear around another curve right away, but I've zeroed in on them. A mysterious beast with five backs that I was sure had to exist – and now, as a reward for tribulations whose onset I can no longer recall, I'm allowed to see it.

I'm climbing my way up to the head of the race.

A curve, I see them again. Suddenly there's a gap between the front two and the back two. The car has pulled over to one side, we pass them. We're passing two dumped riders: Sanchez and the guy in the Molteni jersey. They're out of the saddle, they're going to try to catch a wheel. In front of us Boutonnet and Teissonnière. Four, can that be right? There has to be another rider up in front, otherwise the race director's car would be here. Oh yeah, the rider from Cycles Goff.

When we get to within twenty meters of Boutonnet and Teissonnière, Lebusque picks up the pace. It's not an attack, he's not capable of that, he's just strangling us slowly. Kléber drops back to sit on Lebusque's wheel. I'm on Kléber's. Barthélemy drops back to my side. This is the crunch: anyone who's not in on this one isn't going to win. I fill in the rattle of bikes and voices around me; all I know is Kléber's back wheel. I shift: forty-three seventeen. A couple of kicks which my calves are obviously not thrilled about, pain in my lungs and in the rest. But pain, commonly seen in my circles as a signal to stop doing something, has ceased being that to me ever since July 20, 1972. Kléber's legs are visibly spattering all over the place. I think: butcher. All adjoining parts of my brain – the tactile part, the olfactory, the computing center – are brought in to help think: butcher, butcher. Lebusque is tearing the race apart.

Kilometer 72. Right when I think, now I have to quit, Lebusque slows down. He looks around to survey what he's done.

Kléber slides up next to him. Kléber and Lebusque are in the lead, I'm riding third. I go back to the forty-three nineteen. Coppi, Bartali, Lebusque, Kléber, I've never felt their pain, I'm the only rider in the world whose pain I've ever felt; that makes me a pretty unique individual.

I look around too, but counting things behind me is too hard. I see only the green of Reilhan, and I know Barthélemy must have been dropped. Gradually, a rhythm descends on me again. But rhythm is no longer enough to muffle the pain. Maybe a little mental arithmetic. I know one: what's forty-three divided by nineteen?

Jesus Christ. The nineteen walks over to the glass of forty-three, takes two slugs, wipes its mouth, rubs its chin thoughtfully, stands there like that for a few minutes and then turns to the audience with furrowed brow, arms raised in surrender.

Forty-three divided by twenty, that would be a lot easier, wouldn't it?

One more kilometer to climb. Huddled together, we carry our pain uphill. I look back and catch a glimpse of Barthélemy, twenty meters behind us. When I look again, he's closer. He's been dumped, but he's coming back. Character.

Another kilometer. Gnash, roll, behind Lebusque and Kléber.

A hundred meters in front of us, a group is standing along the road. They see us. They crouch down a little, a smile of collective pleasure appearing on their faces. They clench their fists, sweep them above the road, shout to us. '*Allez, Poupou.*'

I look at a girl in the group. She's sixteen, she's pretty. '*Allez, les sportifs,*' she shouts. '*Un deux un deux.*'

Why is she shouting that?

She knows Hinault fell into a ravine, but not the names of

the classics he won. Classics? She knows everything about Poupou, but she's never heard of Milan–San Remo, has no idea what a forty-three nineteen is.

What gives this girl the right to raise her voice?

In the two of us she sees the twin exponents of the Coke-It's-The-Real-Thing equation. She's the generation that no longer cheers for the riders, but for the journalistic cliché she recognizes in them. Now that I'm five centimeters closer, I can see how pretty she really is. I hate her.

For her, road racing no longer exists. Road racing has gone into the cement mixer of journalism and come out again as the courage of the lone rider, as Poupou, doping doping, today the *domestique* must shine, Simpson on Mont Ventoux.

She belongs to the generation of emblems. She thinks I got my bicycle out of that cement mixer, that it's an emblem I use to identify myself as a proponent of the 'fitness' rage, like her, with her sweatshirt with the TRAINING decal on it. OK, she's not wearing it right now, but I'm sure it's hanging in her closet. If she has a bicycle, it's definitely a 'ten-speed'; if she ever rides it, then it's in the lowest gear possible, hands down on the bottom of the bars. And if she has a milkman, then he wears a sweater saying UNIVERSITY OF OHIO. I hate her.

Never will I be able to make clear to her that I don't race because I wanted to lose weight, because turning thirty horrified me, because I was dissatisfied with café life, because I wanted to write this book, or because of anything else at all, but purely and simply because it's road racing. And even if she believed that, how much less could I make her see that

60

I've got a smidgen of what it takes, without her thinking that I'd been lying in that ravine beside Hinault.

'Hey, pretty girl, I came in seventeenth in the Milan–San Remo.'

'Seventeenth? How many came in after you?'

Really, if I want that pretty girl to understand me, there's only one thing I can do: become champion of the world.

Kilometer 72–73. Painted on the road, in white letters: ML COL 500. That means I can expect this climb to end somewhere within the next two hundred meters to a kilometer, and that the *Midi Libre* once passed this way. This is racy countryside: every crossing has its four faded white arrows, to show riders the way. If my memory serves me, the climb lasts another three hundred meters from this point.

I've run through the calculations a few times, and now I know for sure: there can only be one man out in front, the rider from Cycles Goff. No idea how far ahead he is. After looking around three times I've established that there are six of us here. Lebusque and Kléber in front, me behind them, then Barthélemy, who has indeed come back, then Reilhan and Teissonnière. The boy in the Molteni jersey and Sanchez couldn't hold us. Boutonnet must have been dropped when Lebusque picked up the pace. Of the original seven-man break, only two are left. The race is assuming its definitive form. What Barthélemy is doing is really something, I've got to admit.

Lebusque and Kléber in front. Lebusque standing on the pedals, taking big steps that cut through everything. The man's not a rider, he's a *factor*. Kléber, grinding away evenly, hasn't been out of the saddle all day. The way that guy hangs in there in races like this!

Kilometer 73. A curve. Past the curve I see open space. The end of the woods and the end of the climb.

Kléber sprints to the line for the *Midi Libre*. He crosses it first, five lengths ahead of the rest. Probably because he's so bad on the downhill stretches, because he wants to follow my example and be the first to start the descent. He's forgotten that this is a plateau.

○

Kilometer 74. The Causse Noir. A cold wind comes in at an angle and hits us in the face. Unlimited visibility over rolling, light-green fields. Dark sky to the left and the hills that hide Mont Aigoual.

And suddenly I see, half a kilometer in front of me, two slow-moving cars with a rider between them. The rider from Cycles Goff, the lead rider in the Tour de Mont Aigoual, the last rider we still had to see.

The wind is coming from the right now, blowing hard. I swing to that side, to form a pace line. 'Come on, guys. A little co-operation, we'll be with him like that!' I shout.

I move up to point position, to set the good example. If there's one thing Dutchmen know how to do, it's form a pace line. I look ahead to find a point where I'll end my pull, and am just eyeing a low wall when Lebusque passes me.

Kilometer 74–75. Now we're trading off. Whenever I move up to the front, I look at the rider from Cycles Goff. He has a little less than a minute's lead. He's not cycling in a straight line – the wind seizes him and lets him go again – but his style is still impeccable. How long has he been on his own? One by one, my cronies slide past me: Kléber, Reilhan, Teissonnière, Lebusque. Can that be right? I look back; no, Barthélemy hasn't been dropped, he's sitting on the last wheel, refusing to do his bit.

We rotate, and as I glide past Teissonnière I ask him where the rider from Cycles Goff made his jump. I have to ask twice before he understands my question, and only three turns after that can I make out his answer: 'On the way down.'

Together the five of us struggle against a wall of wind. Pulling the lead, dropping back to the rear, then the hardest moment of all – catching a wheel in the lee, then moving back up through that lee to the front. We work together without a word, but not Barthélemy.

He's hanging onto the tail, he's dogging it.

There is, of course, only one group with as little use for my achievements as the pretty girl. I discovered that on the evening of July 26, 1975.

Earlier that day I'd ridden number 224, a 120-kilometer road race in Berlare, in Belgium. I was a force to be reckoned with that day, there amid the up-and-coming Merckx's and De Vlaemincks. I was up front the whole time, and made no less than twelve fantastic jumps, straight into the wind, to the wrong break. 'Who in the world is that demon in the white jersey?' wondered all those up-and-coming Merckx's and De Vlaemincks.

Strangely enough, I'd just allowed myself to drop back to the middle of the bunch when the real tussle began. So many clusters of riders had formed in front of me, all chasing one another, that anyone who wanted to have a chance clearly had to be in on this *now*, and risk making the jump on his own.

I jumped.

I fought my way into the wind; across the cobblestones of a village where women stood talking to the garbage man I chased the riders in front of me, past a shuttered café, around corners where old Belgians with red-rimmed signs stood waiting. On straight, muck-filled stretches of road I'd sometimes see all those clusters at the same time. They started blending together. Me on my own, against all of them. I bent to the bars in a cramp of exertion. Everything, Timmy, give it everything. Just a little more. Every once in a while I raised my head. Each time I saw that I was a little closer. But I wasn't there yet, I had to go on. I couldn't do it any more, but I had to go on. Body and spirit shook hands and moved to their corners. I looked: closer once more. But still a gap. Suddenly I realized that I'd been wrong: I would never make it by any normal means. I had the extremely simple choice of either giving up (but then never racing again) or going straight through everything that was me. I went through. I'd never drawn that deeply on myself; I was way past the point where I'd cracked before. There was no turning back. And every time I looked up, I was closer. I could already smell the cozy, soothing odor of balsam on their legs. I wanted to shout to them, wait for me, but first I wanted to formulate that idea in perfect clarity. I thought: *way*! and knew that wasn't quite it, but it was as far as I could get.

Retrospectively, my whole life had had only one goal: making that last wheel, here, now. I was wasted. But that elusive finish line, eight, seven, six-and-a-half meters in front of me, kept my hope and my desire awake. I coughed and slobbered. I remembered the words of advice: 'Shift, when you're really, truly at the end of your rope, to a higher gear.' I shifted. A few hysterical kicks on the thirteen, the clenched power of a mortal struggle. I was there. I was sitting on that last wheel. I was in the lead group.

I was in the lead group for one sweep of the cranks, then I was dumped. The blind wall of wind was there again for me alone. What kind of nonsense is this? I thought, then the lights went out.

When a runner faints, his will sees to it that that happens after the finish line. That's how it's been since the soldier of Marathon. The runner has the added advantage of a finish line which, when he can go no further, will also go no further, while I, the rider, had to cope with a finish line that took advantage of my powerlessness to make its escape. On the other hand, to my advantage was that I only had to stay linked to consciousness through one little crack to keep myself upright and rolling on.

I rolled on. Dumped. One meter or a hundred meters; in any event, irrevocably. I'd been there for one sweep of the cranks. But they didn't want me. I'd given up a few thousand hours of my life to prove that I belonged with them, and now it turned out that this was not the case.

I had to stop racing.

After I'd been rolling like that for about ten seconds, two men on bikes passed me. Working in harmony, they seemed out to catch the group of riders in front of us. In some unclear fashion I managed to hook up with them. I didn't do my work, and bore a great deal of abuse. After some time, during which I went deeper than I had ever gone before, it appeared that we had joined the lead group. A good thirty minutes later, with one lap to go before the finish, I was able to count the members of our group. Twenty. During a long, straight stretch, I looked back. At least a kilometer behind us rode the bunch. Dumpees. Nanny goats.

During the final lap, three riders escaped from our group. Five hundred meters before the finish I attacked, in an attempt to come in fourth. I gave it everything I had, but it wasn't enough. Two hundred meters before the finish they caught up with me again. Virtually the whole group rode right over me. I came in nineteenth.

Because we were going to race in Belgium again the next day, my friend and I went to stay near the border with a friend of his, the racer Gerard Koel. A lot of Dutch riders live around there, because it makes it easier for them to race in Belgium; Knetemann, Kuiper, Koel, Jan Janssen. And Harm Ottenbros, the world champion on the road for professionals in 1969 and at that time, in 1975, still one of the top Dutch riders, a man feared for his awesome sprint. That evening we ended up at his house. I had to go along, even though, to stay in form, I would rather have turned in early.

Ottenbros was very friendly. 'A brew, gentlemen?' he said, already on his way to the fridge. He came back with four bottles of beer. Since the start of my road-racing career I'd stopped drinking beer, but somehow that seemed too complicated to explain. So I drank along with Ottenbros, my first beer in two-and-a-half years.

Ottenbros asked what we'd done that day. Raced. How had it gone? My buddy said: 'I missed the jump.'

Then it was my turn. I hadn't missed the jump. I'd been in the lead group, and I'd come in nineteenth.

'The lead? Nineteenth?' Ottenbros said.

That's right, nineteenth in a field of at least a hundred up-and-coming Merckx's and De Vlaemincks! And I began to explain what had gone wrong with my final spurt. How I'd given it my all, in an attempt to come in fourth! And I hadn't made it! Even though I was usually one of the better sprinters; on the average, I came in sixth in that kind of sprint.

When I'd finished my story, no one said a thing.

The silence lasted for a while, then talk gradually resumed, again about racing. Koel and Ottenbros were doing most of the talking now. I was handed another beer and looked around the room. On the wall was a framed certificate, with a drawing of the globe and a little rider on it. The certificate said that Ottenbros had been world road champion in 1969.

I listened. The feeling grew stronger that, just because

these people were big shots in the world of racing, they still had no right to speak about it with such aplomb.

Ottenbros saw me sitting there, staring, and tried to draw me back into the group with a few questions about my racing career. I answered them.

'So, you're taking a stab at it, are you?' he said amiably. 'But aren't you Tim Krabbé, the chess player?'

Kilometer 75–78. The fields are a dry yellow and light green. Endless fences lean crookedly across the landscape. To keep something out of the wind? The road is narrow and rolling. Uphill or down, you can't sort it out, it drives you crazy. We shift, we stand on the pedals when we get too lazy to shift again. The sky up ahead is black. No one is watching us. More than two hours to go.

The rider from Cycles Goff is ahead of us, on his own, a hero in the cold land. We don't advance on him and he doesn't advance away from us. He'll never keep that up; if he has any sense he'll drop back. Is it true, by the way, that the music I hear is coming from the race director's car?

One by one they slide past me, on their way to work up front, and then back through the lee to the rear. A sentence for my racing logbook formulates itself: 'Pace line worked together passably well.' That's laying it on thick. The pulls are irregular and the steering's bad; they're better at this back in Holland.

Lebusque blows his nose. A spatter lands on my thigh, the rest on the Causse Noir. He takes pulls that are three

68

times as long as the others'. I don't understand the man. Later on he'll crack and get dumped. There we have Reilhan, sitting pretty, not a single word on the inside of his forehead. He's dogging it, his father would be proud. Teissonnière is staring off endlessly into space, or else at Reilhan's back wheel, I can't tell. Kléber looks worried, here in the wind. He only tolerates the wind because he knows mountains are coming later on. Little holes all over his bike: like lots of riders, he spends hours drilling out his parts; removing morsels of weight wherever he can. 'Ever thought about how much extra wind resistance that creates, Stani?' 'Yeah, it's less.'

Reilhan drops back to his father's car and returns with a piece of silver foil, from which he begins slurping up a pretty unattractive looking slop. I wish him a sincere *bon appetit*. He looks at me in bewilderment.

Barthélemy doesn't show his face. Am I supposed to put up with that?

I think they're all still going strong, but of course that's because I don't know what to look for. Ab Geldermans tells about how, when he was Jan Janssen's team director in the Tour de France, he was able to signal to Jan, during climbs for instance, that one of his rivals was scraping bottom. Jan would pick up the pace a little and have one less rival. Road racing imitates life, the way it would be without the corruptive influence of civilization. When you see an enemy lying on the ground, what's your first reaction? To help him to his feet.

In road racing, you kick him to death.

Kilometer 78. Lanuéjols. A village, appearing suddenly out of a wrinkle in the plateau. The smell of manure, farmers on a low wall, a dog that jumps around in its kennel and then begins a ferocious sprint in our direction, rudely interrupted by the tautening of its chain.

Forgetfulness.

Kilometer 78–82. Barthélemy still hanging on the last wheel. He's saving his strength back there; I could have come up with that one myself. He's worried about the next climb: every pull in the wind he avoids here gets him one more meter before being dropped later on. If he keeps this up, he'll actually get a chance or two, the sweat-thief.

When I swing to the back of the group, I turn and look at him.

'The wind's blowing pretty hard here, Barthélemy, how about it?'

No response. I'm violating the rule that we're no longer speaking to each other. His hands are clenched around his brakehoods, his legs grind away, his spectacles are a blindfold.

'Barthélemy, you maybe a little tired? You not know my number yet?'

No response. I take my turn up front and look around at him again when I get back.

'Barthélemy, the wind is blowing for you, too!'

Nothing. He sits there like a block of granite from which a rider may later be hewn. If I keep this up, I'll get myself a smack in the face. That coalition of ours, of course, was only the first step on the way to the fight we should have had long ago. From one moment to the next, every action could be interpreted as betrayal. The first little vendettas were carried out with a wink, I made openings for Teissonnière, he sicked his *domestiques* on me, and before we knew it we were grimly blowing each other's attacks to pieces. On two occasions, Reilhan won races in which Barthélemy and I finally had to fight out a battle of prestige for tenth place.

The long-awaited eruption of our grudge took place during race 302, on May 15, 1977. I had betrayed him! He had betrayed me! He exploded, he howled. If I felt like a punch in the nose right there, all I had to do was say so. Better yet, we could get off and slug it out on the spot!

With that our feud became a matter of fact, and from that moment on we could start giving each other a little more room to breathe. But feud or no feud, Barthélemy has no right to save his energy at our expense. Kléber looks back and I signal to him to move up in my place.

I pedal on, but slower. I let the group get ahead. Lebusque looks back, Teissonnière looks back, Reilhan looks back: they're missing me in the pace line.

There. He wasn't expecting that one.

I move all the way to the left side of the road, to let him catch as much wind as possible. The gap grows and grows, but Barthélemy sticks to my wheel. Road racing is a sport of patience. If the bastard wants to win this race, now he has a chance to show it.

We're behind by fifty meters.

Tour of Flanders, 1976. After Paris–Roubaix, the Tour of Flanders is the most important of the one-day classics. In 1976, the two strongest riders in that field were the Belgians Freddy Maertens and Roger De Vlaeminck: neither of them had ever won the Tour of Flanders.

After 160 kilometers, the lead group consisted of five men: Walter Planckaert, Moser, Demeyer, Maertens and De Vlaeminck. There were still a hundred kilometers left to the finish – for ninety-five of them, the escapees worked together well. Close to the end Moser tried to jump several times, but was always caught. When he tried it again five kilometers before the finish, Demeyer and Planckaert jumped with him, but De Vlaeminck, with Maertens on his wheel, let them go.

Maertens and De Vlaeminck were bitter rivals.

'De Vlaeminck is the one who let them go,' Maertens figured quite rightly. 'So it's up to him to bridge the gap.'

He waited. The gap grew and grew.

'He wants to win, so let him bridge the gap,' thought Maertens.

'He wants to win, so let him bridge the gap,' thought De Vlaeminck.

Both of them knew that the one who finally bridged the gap would use up energy to his rival's benefit. What mattered now was: staying patient.

Both riders stayed patient: bravo! The winner of the 1976 Tour of Flanders was Walter Planckaert.

Oh, the wondrous powers in a man that only come to light thanks to rivalry!

World Championship Road Racing, 1948. Who would win, Coppi or Bartali? Coppi and Bartali were the strongest riders of their day.

It was a thrilling race, with many an interesting development. Kübler and Clemens left the peloton: Coppi and Bartali looked at each other. Dupont, Ricci and Schotte left the peloton: Coppi and Bartali looked at each other. Caput, Teissière and Lazaridès left the peloton: Coppi and Bartali looked at each other. Schulte and Ockers left the peloton: Coppi and Bartali looked at each other.

When the peloton at last consisted only of Coppi and Bartali, they looked at each other and climbed off, both of them satisfied, we might assume, with a success sweeter than the sweetest second place. The Italian racing federation suspended them both for two months.

Fifty meters, a hundred. Can spectacles wink?

I look straight ahead: Reilhan looks around and rides up to the front of the four. I wait for Barthélemy's inevitable jump, the one that will bring me back. No jump comes. This is making me awfully nervous: Doesn't he want to win?

Oh yes, De Vlaeminck hated to die, but Maertens' death was worth it. Maertens was right, but his mistake was in trying to prove it. As the better sprinter, he was the favorite, and the favorite has to accept that he's the one open to blackmail.

What am I doing, for God's sake? Did Coppi ever drop back to rob Mortimer Snerd of the victory? Isn't my defeat the best thing Barthélemy could hope to achieve today?

I come up out of the saddle, I shift and jump, Barthélemy on my wheel. I bite in the hard air, I rip down the left side of the road, I bridge the gap at a single tug. Now what to do with my velocity? I could always use it to make my brake blocks nice and toasty: little shavings will go flying off them, my bike another thousandth of a gram lighter.

In a flash I size up the openings on both sides of the bunch. I choose the smallest one, give it a few extra pushes and hiss through. Maybe Barthélemy will have to hit his brakes. 'Ho hey, ho hey,' Reilhan shouts, but his voice isn't a lasso, I'm flying into open space.

I'm gone. Unbelievable, the rashness with which bicycle races are sometimes decided. For a while I see nothing and feel nothing either, I've been transformed into my own body.

I can't see the rider from Cycles Goff, but the team car hiding him keeps getting bigger. And then it swings to one side. There's the lead man. He's coming up out of the saddle to go with me.

I pass him.

My sporting career: 1958

A Dutchman had won the Tour! It was Charly Gaul. In fact he was a Luxembourger, but he rode in the combined Dutch–Luxembourg team, and in Paris I had personally seen him enter the Parc des Princes. I was standing outside, by the gate, and the whole peloton came in as one. I looked for the yellow of Gaul, saw it flash by and noted his look of satisfaction.

Shortly afterwards I saw him again, at Amsterdam's Olympic Stadium, when the Nelux team was making its tribute appearance. The newspaper story claiming that Gaul had asked for and received money to show up at the ceremony seemed illogical to me. Seated in a horse-drawn carriage, Gaul circled the cinder track. I cheered for him and tried to imagine what he was feeling.

After that the Nelux riders and a few others rode a 'mini-Tour'. It was a points race with twenty-four sprints, one for each stage that had been ridden in that Tour de France. Gaul cycled along calmly in the bunch and didn't get involved in the attacks. That made sense, because in the early stages of a Tour the favorites always stayed calm. Then came the thirteenth sprint. In the Tour, the thirteenth stage had been the first one in the mountains; the speaker announced that all of today's sprints corresponding to mountain stages in the Tour were *mountain* sprints. Just like in the Tour, they were tougher and worth more than the others. This was reflected by the points being doubled. I kept a sharp eye on Gaul, who was still staying calm. Come on, Charly, I thought, this is your forte, this is where you can nail them.

In the days that followed I decided to practice riding time trials. The mountains were more important, but there weren't any mountains nearby, and time trials came immediately after that.

I put my chess clock on the windowsill and took off. I gave it everything I had. Everything. 'Hey, Speedy,' boys along the street yelled. I had twenty sugar cubes with me, because Gaul always ate lots of sugar cubes during stages, too.

Along the way I was passed regularly by other riders. Mostly by Anquetil, even though he'd sometimes started more than ten minutes after me. But his bike was a lot better, and I was only fifteen. I rode till I burst. Time trials are a battle against yourself. I never coasted behind motor scooters; Anquetil never did that either.

I had developed a technique of hopping off the bike at full speed in front of the house and landing precisely in front of the window where my clock was, so I could note my time as quickly as possible. One entire cerebral lobe is still reserved for my record: 46 minutes and 53 seconds. Once I'd read the clock I would remain leaning over my handlebars for a few minutes, until I had enough strength to put the key in the lock. After that I would lie on my bed for fifteen minutes. 'Tim has gone nuts,' my brother would say when he saw me like that.

One time someone had taken the clock away.

The distance covered in my time trial was 22.5 kilometers. My average was therefore 28.794881 k.p.h. Not bad for a fifteen-year-old boy on a street bike without gears, a boy who had to watch out at intersections, sometimes wait for traffic lights, who wore an anorak and long pants instead of rider's gear, and who, during record attempts at dusk, had to supply the power for a humming dynamo as well. (And who knows, maybe my average was even higher that time the clock had been taken away.)

I wanted to be a road racer. I inquired about racing clubs and equipment, but no one I knew could tell me how to go about it. I wanted a paper route, to save for a racing bike, but the very first newspaper I applied to didn't need any paper-boys. So I started using my chess clock for chess again. Pity, really: how wonderful it might have been, a chess grand-master who also rode in the Tour de France.

(When, after turning thirty, I became a bicycle racer after all, I tried to demolish that fifteen-year-old boy's record. I left from the same spot, the traffic lights were favorable, I rode my guts out. But when I tried to take the turn to the right, the one that led onto the country road, I couldn't find any road to the right. Where the fields had been were now tall apartment buildings. I looked at them, panting. I recognized the feeling – the clock had been taken from the windowsill. I nodded to myself: it didn't seem unreason-able.)

Kilometer 82. After two hours and twenty-nine minutes of cycling, my front wheel is the first in the Tour de Mont Aigoual. I like to do that during the first few kilometers, but today Despuech beat me to it.

'Two escapees join the lone lead rider,' Roux announces to the void of the Causse Noir. 'It's Krabbé of Anduze and Barthélemy of Alès.'

The rider from Cycles Goff passes me again. The decisive escape! '*Allez*,' I hiss at him. A drop blows in my face, too cold to be his sweat.

I pass him, I'm really hammering in the lead, into the wind. Behind me no sound of an argument: it seems Cycles Goff can live with the presence of our sweat-thief.

The Tour de Mont Aigoual has entered a new phase. A

lead group of three: Krabbé, Cycles Goff, Barthélemy. Followed at fifteen seconds, maybe more, by four riders: Reilhan, Kléber, Lebusque, Teissonnière.

All the others are out of it.

Kilometer 83. Each time the rider from Cycles Goff glides by me, I look at him. He's young and he's beautiful. And even though he's been riding solo for the last hour, he's sitting easy. Class. You know what, let's make him eighteen years of age and the future winner of oodles of stages in the Tour de France. This was his amateur career, about which he never went into detail later on. When he won his first stage, the Saturday supplement published a story of mine entitled 'I Rode with the Rider from Cycles Goff', in which I emphasized the class he had shown at eighteen, and which I had recognized even then. In the Tour de Mont Aigoual of 1977, I had been the only one of fifty-two riders who had managed to stay on his wheel.

The drop that's fallen on my thigh now is a raindrop. No house, no farm in sight. Bare and cold. In the foreword to one of his novels, Jean Carrière says of high plateaux like these that, even in 1950, some of the Catholic inhabitants thought Huguenots had only one eye, in the middle of their foreheads.

The race has entered a new phase, and every thirty seconds my wheel is in the lead, but is this a sensible phase as far as I'm concerned? Aren't I in the process of letting myself be jerked around by Barthélemy again?

I'm the one up pushing in the wind, and that's helping *his* odds for the third climb. Odds he'll be able to double during the descent. He'll get dumped later on, but perhaps so late that he'll be able to come back after the climb. The further I take him, the greater the chance that the toughest race of the season will be won by a bad climber.

I'm an ass.

This escape has to be made undone. What was stupid at first is now the best thing to do. I drop back to second position and slow down. I stop pedaling. The rider from Cycles Goff misses me taking my turn and looks back, puzzled. The gap is ten meters. I look over my shoulder. When I turn back around, Barthélemy jumps and passes me, very powerfully. He goes right past Cycles Goff, who makes a reflex move to follow, then drops back on his saddle.

Barthélemy is already a hundred meters out in front.

The rider from Cycles Goff lets himself glide back beside me. We look back. We see the four.

'Still too far,' I say.

He hesitates for a second, then nods.

'Right, suicide.'

We straighten up, drift along, fifteen seconds to breathe just for the fun of it.

Kilometer 84. New situation in the Tour de Mont Aigoual: Barthélemy in the lead, then thirty seconds after him a group of six, consisting of: Teissonnière, Krabbé, Kléber, Lebusque, Reilhan and the rider from Cycles Goff.

The team car from Alès passes us. It's going with Barthélemy. Ridiculous. Kléber's chances are much better. If he punctures now, God knows how long he'll have to wait.

The black plume hanging to the top of Mont Aigoual looks like it's got blacker. A fat, cold drop falls down the back of my neck and ten others blow in my face at the same time.

○

Kilometer 84–88. A *faux plat* going down fails to swell back up again, adding speed to my speed: the high plateau is over, the descent to the bottom of a new gorge has begun.

Trèves: five kilometers and falling.

My tactics! I ride to the front, shoot my way around the yellow lights of an oncoming car. I lick my lips. Sand and salt. Branches on the road, red mud. It's not the rain that's taken us by surprise; it could have been raining here for the last hundred years. We've ridden *into* the rain.

I'd been descending between two safe patches of pasture-land, but they go away, a rock wall takes the place of one, nothing takes the place of the other. I would be extremely grateful right now if someone projected a dot of light out in front of me, to show exactly how fast you can go here. I'm quite willing to tough it out at this point, but preferably within the limits of the competent, otherwise they'll all be looking down on me again. Aha: a sign: maximum speed 60 k.p.h. Shall I point to it and waggle my finger in warning at the others? I'm not the man who invented the wheel first, I'm the one who invented it most often.

A curve, I flinch, almost brake, brake, my back wheel skids out from under me, I stop braking, stay upright. Boy oh boy. I roll on, pull my feet out of the toe-clips so I can drag them over the ground if necessary. We Dutch bear the mark. There is a sociologically pinpointable group of Dutch people who, when I tell them that I race, react with a knowing wink and that famous slogan: 'Wim van Est fell into a deep ravine, his heart stopped ticking, but his Pontiac watch was fine.' This one's deeper. What, for example, must one do when both brakes jam during a descent? In such cases, Wim van Est braked with his hand on his front tire, and if that didn't help he stuck his foot in the spokes. Wim van Est was a cartoon character.

I ride in the middle of the road as much as I can: that makes it harder to get by me.

Lebusque gets by me, Reilhan gets by me, the rider from Cycles Goff gets by me, Teissonnière gets by me. They're swallowed up by the darkness in front of me, they disappear around boulders.

Kléber gets by me.

Why don't they ever organize *downhill* time trials? The climbers have their uphill trials, so why shouldn't the downhill men have downhill trials? It's because public opinion would be against riders toying with their lives just to gain a few seconds. Which is precisely what they do anyway, but then muffled away in a much larger whole.

81

Death is a *vedette*, but we like him to keep his appearances functional.

1 2 3 4 5 6 7 8 9 10 11 12 13 14 15 16 17 18 19 20 21 22 23 24 25 26 27 28 29 30 31 32 33 34 35 36 37 38 39 40 41 42 43 44 45 46 47 48 49 50 51 52 53 54 55 56 57 58 59 60 61 62 63 64 65 66 67 68 69 70 71 72 73 74 75 76 77 78 79 80 81 82 83 84 85 86 87 88 89 90 91 92 93 94 95 96 97 98 99 100: numbers worn by riders killed in races.

I bear down after a curve: cramp.

I've been working hard, I'm sweaty, but now I have to sit in this cold wind without moving. The faster I go, the more it hurts to sit still. My hands feel sharp, my legs want to ride. The slower I go, the worse I get dumped.

There's someone in a purple jersey lying along the road. He's holding his head in his hands and shouting something full of 'o's. A few meters further his bike is leaning against a rock, more or less the way a tourist would park it when stopping to eat a sandwich.

I know only one person with a bicycle and a purple jersey: Teissonnière. He must have fallen, his bike bounced back and came to a stop against that rock. Doesn't matter, I don't need Teissonnière any more.

My legs go wobbly with fright for him.

Race 177, March 15, 1975. I'd been training all winter, my body was cycling right out from under my warm-ups. I wanted to go racing in Belgium as soon as possible, but the drizzly weather put the others off, as did the name of the place I planned to ride: Zichem-Keiberg. So I went alone. Holland and Belgium were indeed packed boundlessly in a cold, gray rain cloud.

Zichem-Keiberg was of clay. Whatever they hadn't needed for their houses and stables was left lying on the road. The things and the sky blended together with no clear border. I picked up my number in a café called 'Gust and Jackie's Place'. There were 130 other riders, and with that as peloton we left from the café for twelve nine-kilometer circuits through the clay. Rain came from everywhere and went everywhere. After a hundred meters, the first riders rattled to the ground. After one kilometer my feet were squishing in my shoes at every stroke; a jet of mud from the wheel in front of me squirted me between the eyes.

As the name of the town had indicated, a considerable part of the route consisted of *keien*, cobbles. Belgium's cobblestone roads were, as some Amsterdam riders put it, 'built by the Romans, who just dumped a bunch of rocks out of a helicopter'. On the cobbles a man finds out what it is to be a jackhammer. Your arms grow three times as thick, your jaws clatter like castanets, your chain starts chattering and would like nothing more than to go flying off. But anyway. During the very first lap I myself had become the border between the things and the sky. I took on shin guards of clay, and my *bidon* contained a mixture of yogurt drink, raisin cookies and clay. I thought, I'll never get out of here, but I was content with that. This was bicycle racing. The real racing, the thing I'd been looking for so long. I gave everything I had to give,

83

and that was just enough not to get dropped. I thought: Close my eyes and go to sleep, close my eyes and go to sleep. I had vanished into road racing.

By the halfway point, seventy of the 130 riders were left, and I was one of them. No matter how small that peloton became, I was always going to stay with it.

At that same point, I saw a rider up in front make his escape. From his jersey, I could tell that it was a Dutchman. To keep too many others from following, he swung hard to the left. He looked back to see whether his plan had worked, and slammed head-on into an oncoming car. He bounced away like a leaky ball. He flew through the air and landed with a smack in the middle of the peloton he'd been so eager to leave. A few other riders fell too, either struck by this airborne attack or trying to avoid a collision. I was far enough back to be able to go around them, I saw the escapee lying on the ground. 'Ooooh! Ooooh! Ooooh!' he was crying.

The peloton slowed its pace. Everyone was thinking about Monseré, the young world champion who had died a few years earlier in exactly the same accident. I thought: if they announce that that rider is dead, I'm going to get off my bike. Pain isn't a signal to quit, fear isn't either, but there are things a rider senses he is free to regard as circumstances beyond his control.

After about another lap, the fear had left the legs and the *peloton* was going as fast as ever. The car, a few dents in its black paintjob, stood there for another three or four laps, then it was gone. Finally there were no more than forty riders clustered together at the start of the final lap. I was one of them. For the first time, I joined in an escape; for a moment my wheel was the first in the race. But it ended up in a mass sprint. I was able to think up enough excuses not to have to take part. Too dangerous. The finish line was at the top of the hill of cobbles, and cobbles become slick as butter in the rain. My legs were too stiff. Belgian juries never see Dutch riders in a mass sprint anyway. And the best I could hope for was seventh place – how long before I might run into someone who knew how good that was?

The friendly farmer in whose pigsty I was allowed to change my gear could tell me nothing about what had happened to that rider. I took my number back to Gust and Jackie's, but no one there seemed to want to talk about it. I drove back to Amsterdam. That next Monday I bought a Belgian newspaper. On the cycling page, the first article to catch my eye bore the headline: RIDER KILLED IN RACE. It was about a different race. A young man had skidded in a curve and struck his head against a post.

A few weeks later, in a completely different context in a Dutch cycling magazine, I read that my injured rider had only broken his leg in two places. Later that season he was riding again, and some time later he became the young pro Johan van der Meer, who rode for Jet Star Jeans.

(For a surprisingly long time I kept thinking: the race at Zichem-Keiberg was a week ago today; the race at Zichem-Keiberg was three weeks ago; and, even as I'm writing, it's been no more than a month since the race at Zichem-

Keiberg – but then all my 350 races taken together are the most recent year of my life.)

Kilometer 88–89. Teissonnière out of the race – after eighty-eight kilometers, the Tour de Mont Aigoual has six riders in the lead. I'm number six. I shiver.

A kilometer stone. I can't make out what it says, but it reminds me that I'm further than I was before. Just a little more. Then I will have made it through the two toughest descents of the day without an accident.

A hairpin turn. I brake. I push on and feel a slight cramp. It's the rain, nothing serious.

Kilometer 89. A straight stretch down and I'm there. Trèves. At the entrance to the village stands a farmer with a deadpan face and a pitchfork in his hand. He signals for me to go straight on. Across from him, sitting on a wall, are four old men. I nod to them and murmur: 'Battoowoo Greekgreek.'

'Battoowoo Greekgreek,' they say, tapping a finger to the brim of their caps.

✿

Kilometer 89–90. I shift, lay my wrists next to each other on the bars and pump. Climbing. This one will last *fifteen* kilometers. In front of me, a few racers seem stuck to the new slope, tiny as dots and graspable. Pain in my legs. For a long time there I thought that riders were pawns on bikes, but that's turned out to be a misconception.

86

Pain.

But I must.

These fifteen kilometers carry us to the village of Camprieu, 546 meters above here. That's not as steep as the last two climbs, but that doesn't make it easier – on climbs like this, every gear is either too low or too high.

At Camprieu I may just have to sprint for those two premiums.

Kilometer 90–91. Forty-three seventeen. I'm getting warmer. I'm becoming a cyclist again, and not a bad one at that. In front of me, Cycles Goff and Kléber are riding together, and in front of them Reilhan, on his own. A dangerous situation. If Kléber is able to gather the others around him and I'm not there, I'm done for. That gap has to be bridged right *now*. Not too quickly, not too slowly either: the effort must be minimal. By looking at my hands, how they grip the bars, by means of pure concentration, I can think that my legs are a silent motor with free power, the way in a dream you can concentrate and rise up off the ground a little.

I latch onto the back wheel of Cycles Goff. And now stay with them. Behind me the sound of a car approaching slowly: Stéphan? He has his headlights on; I see them reflected in my front rim. That sentence, I use it to make a flywheel in my head, for staying with. 'I've seen your light reflected in my rim.' A nice sentence. I translate it into French, in which, to do something in return, it becomes even nicer: '*J'ai vu ta lumière dans ma jante.*' A rich language, French, that can spare a word like *jante* for a meaning like rim.

87

A disturbing thought: I'm being followed by people who are gliding along warm and motionless, and who may actually be bored to tears.

Kilometer 91. Another thirteen kilometers to climb. When I look ahead again I see Lebusque as well; so he and Reilhan have joined up, and they're not too far in front of us.

Thirty seconds later Kléber has bridged the gap, a group of five is chasing the leader, Barthélemy.

I've forgotten all about Teissonnière.

The old line-up. Kleber on point, half beside him the enormous Lebusque, then me, Reilhan beside and a little behind me, and the rider from Cycles Goff must be on his wheel.

Forty-three seventeen. Camprieu is incredibly far from here.

It seems to be raining less where we are now, but then back there it was me who was raining, by going fast. A river is running down beside us. I saw it when I was training here with Kléber, but past the trees today I see only a gray featherbed. Little streams are trickling down the road itself; Nature is all too pleased to make use of public works.

We are wet.

The woods thicken. It's getting darker. Little muddy paths lead off to the left, into the woods, until you can't see them any more – where to? We climb. This is never going to end.

And then suddenly, like a bolt of lightning, absolutely nothing happens. But then truly, absolutely nothing, it's a moment of panicky fear.

It's already over. Everything goes on doing what it's always done. I know this feeling. I had it at Zichem-Keiberg, more often during bicycle races, very often as a child. It's the first half of a *déjà vu*.

Kilometer 91–92. We ride on. Kléber in the lead. He must be trying to bridge the gap to Barthélemy, a rider from his own club. And why not? Barthélemy never does a thing for him, his whole club never does a thing for Kléber.

I've found a cadence. Another twelve kilometers to Camprieu.

We are wet, cold and dirty. Pick someone at random and put them on a bicycle here, front wheel pointing in the direction of Camprieu, and ten to one they'll dismount and go looking for shelter in the nearest farmhouse. Why are we riding on? If you ask an alpinist why he climbs a mountain he'll reply: 'Because it's there.'

As far as I know, no one has ever pointed out what nonsense that is. The alpinist's will isn't prompted *by* the mountain, it's there even without a mountain. The alpinist's will is not so petty that it needs something as random as the shape of the earth's crust in order to exist. Even if the earth were as flat as a billiard ball, there would still be alpinists: the true alpinists. The true alpinist would actually be ashamed to have his will molded by things of an order as low as mountains. So only one question could rightly be asked of the true alpinist: why do you never climb mountains?

(I know of only one example of true alpinism in a Tour de France. In 1959, Federico Bahamontes, the great Spanish mountain champion, won the Tour. The next year, in the middle of the second stage, he suddenly climbed off his bike. When asked to explain, he said: '*Moi, il est fatigué. Moi, il veut aller à la maison.*')

Kilometer 92–93. Barthélemy. He twists hard, back and forth, he looks over his shoulder, he shifts, his chain rattles across the sprockets in search of the miracle gear that will erase his pain.

When the gap is down to twenty meters, I attack. Shouting, panic, 'Ho hey'. I shoot past Lebusque, past Kléber. 'Ho hey.' I fly past Barthélemy, I'm going at least twice as fast as he is.

I see nothing. I see an image of Barthélemy trying to build up speed. I give it everything I've got, but at the same time I have to make sure it's not completely everything, otherwise they'll roll right over me afterwards. Another twenty strokes of almost completely everything. Linda, see to it that I have slaughtered Barthélemy, and keep me from getting dropped.

Kilometer 93. I slow down. Kléber rides past me. Lebusque rides past me. If one of them attacks *now*, I won't be able to go along. With everything I've got left, I move up to Lebusque's wheel. I stick to it. The attack's over, and I'm still up front with them.

I look back. Reilhan is on my wheel, then a twenty-meter gap, then the rider from Cycles Goff, mangled on his bike, then nothing.

I have crushed Barthélemy.

OK. Now, by kind leave of the rest of this group, I am a rag, draped over my bike. Barthélemy will have about as much use for his sprinting skills today as I will for my knowledge of the game of chess.

Kilometer 93–100. A minute later, the rider from Cycles Goff has caught up with us. In the lead, after ninety-three kilometers of the Tour de Mont Aigoual, with little more than an hour and a half to go, a group of five: Lebusque, Kléber, Krabbé, Reilhan and Cycles Goff.

Another eleven kilometers to climb to Camprieu. The landscape slides past us, steady and wet. This is what they call a *sur place*. We are five men hanging motionless by our fingertips from a high windowsill, waiting until someone has to let go. Occasionally we lick the mud from our lips.

Camprieu 9 km. Damn, it's been that for the last two markers.

Lebusque, Kléber, me. This race has been going on so long, hasn't Lebusque turned forty-three yet? He looks wet. Whatever happened to him to make him want to do this? Strange, those skinny little moneychanger's legs of Kléber's – and something else I'd like to know: why does the pedal go down when you push, instead of you going up? Behind me and to one side, Reilhan, oh well, a friend too. That smile of his, it's diluted by no more than a drop of amazement at how easily it's all going. Class. I have to turn my head to see the rider from Cycles Goff. He's having a hard time. Every kick he gives is by the skin of his teeth, even I can see that. If you threw a penny at him, he'd be out of the race. The Man with the Hammer should give him a whack, strictly on humanitarian grounds.

We pass a muddy little path running into the woods. *Camprieu 9 km.* No, this is never going to end.

Someday someone walks down that muddy little path. It's raining. After many twists and turns through the woods, he ends up in front of a dilapidated building. Above the entrance hangs a sign: MUSÉE DES CHOSES. He goes inside. He finds himself in a room that is completely empty, except for a shelf on a far wall, bearing five jars. He looks at them. Each jar contains a complete set of human brains in formaldehyde. A card is leaning against one of the jars. He reads: 'Brains lead group, Tour de Mont Aigoual, 6/26/77.'

Kilometer 100. I look back. The rider from Cycles Goff is gone.

Kilometer 100–103. Four-man break. In front of me: Lebusque and Kléber, side by side. Don Quixote and Sancho Panza. The builds are right, only the sizes have been switched around. The rain is falling down on us. Our entire audience has gone home. Roux's car plays a happy tune and describes our merits to the wet poppies and two cellophane-wrapped tourists. Our indomitability. He tells them that I'm from Holland, making it sound like there's a motley crew of Hungarians and Puerto Ricans in our wake. Another four kilometers to Camprieu, another four kilometers to climb. Why am I whining about Camprieu? After Camprieu there are two kilometers of flat road, then an eight-kilometer climb. Camprieu is a fallacy, an overgrown kilometer stone. Another four kilometers to Camprieu.

Did I feel that right, has Kléber speeded up just a fraction? Admirable Kléber, who seeks nothing in bicycle racing but to show us his back in the mountains. He doesn't try to escape; beyond the range of our pain he would be lost. Along his lower thighs, a brown juice is trickling down. Has he pissed in his pants? Shit in them? Or is it mud, and do I have that too?

'Hey, Lebusque.'

He looks at me.

'*Lebusque, courir c'est mourir un peu.*'

He growls and looks straight ahead again.

I move up closer to him. '*Gau d'amite, Lebusque, courir c'est mourir un peu!*'

He doesn't get it, mumbles something I don't understand, and turns his head back towards Camprieu.

Beside me: Reilhan. Can it be that Reilhan's smile is no longer precisely the same as always? Reilhan, you're wearing a green jersey.

Indeed, Kléber has speeded up a little. During our test ride, he'd dropped me kilometers ago. He always drops me on the climbs when we're training. As he slides away from me then, a sentence for my cycling log formulates itself: 'Saw no use in following his tempo and let him go.' But during the race I stay with him. Because I *want* to.

93

Cold, rain, kilometers, mud; when I want something, I can do it.

I am a hero, you see.

Kilometer 103. Sign: CAMPRIEU 1 KM. Here and there a house along the road; we're back in the world. That means the climb is almost over: sometimes you reach the end of something only because you forget for a moment that it isn't over yet.

There are two premiums to be won at Camprieu – but where? All we know is that it's 'in Camprieu'. It must be at the top of the climb. We're keeping an eye on one another. Of course none of us is interested in those premiums, but one must see to it that no one else takes them.

And there we go: Reilhan jumps. Kléber looks back nervously, then stands and – in that snappy little style of his – jumps after him, past Lebusque.

I have to go along. My legs feel black and scared. I have to. I can do it. I catch Kléber, I hold him.

My sporting career: 1957
The rider is ready. Every fiber of his body is tensed. The interests at stake here are enormous. He knows the opposition is strong and varied, but he is not afraid. In his mind, all is absolute silence, tension, certainty.

Then the traffic light turns green. Two, three strokes and the rider is spurting full out; there he goes, the first to shoot across the tramline, earning him the usual hundred-thousand-guilder premium. Of all his rivals, a Volkswagen poses the greatest threat, but the rider squeezes out every last drop and succeeds in throwing himself over the front of the crosswalk first, then over the back of the crosswalk, as first past a traffic post *and* as first past a garbage can: four more fat prizes of one hundred thousand guilders each. Then the Volkswagen passes him.

But he's still first among two-wheelers! He passes the back and then the front bumpers of two parked cars, the two curbs of a side street and an advertising kiosk before a scooter catches up with him; by then, however, that's earned him another seven times one thousand guilders.

The rider is about to cut in and coast when he sees up ahead a woman on a bike, with a child on the back. Two hundred thousand guilders if he passes her before she gets to that pole. Two hundred thousand! Even though he's no-where near having recovered from his sprint, the rider jumps again with all his might. No way he can ever beat this woman. But this rider has surprised the sporting world before, and this time he gives it every milli-billimeter he's got: in a desperate attempt, he pitches forward.

The woman sticks out her hand and turns down a side street.

The rider rolls out, slowly catches his breath, cruises up to the next traffic light. He stands and eyes his opponents. The BMW motorcycle seems fairly invincible.

A million if he beats it to the crosswalk anyway!

Kilometer 104. Signpost CAMPRIEU. I'm on Kléber's wheel. Reilhan took off too soon, he's not gaining any more ground. What I expected is exactly what's happening now: Reilhan is going to get crushed as well. Ten meters behind him, Kléber accelerates again. I'm on his wheel. Reilhan can't go with us. A race is being decided here. In a flash, I look back. Only Reilhan, thirty meters behind us now, then nothing. No Lebusque: Lebusque couldn't even answer Kléber's first jump!

Kléber hammers away; this is looking like a full sprint. He shifts and I shift, but it's nothing more than a push of the lever: things here don't get around to having names.

People along the road – the line must be up there, at the top of the climb. Now I'll show Kléber what sprinting really is, and I start passing him, but my legs get such a fright that I grant him the honor.

He's worked hard enough for it, and the premiums are both fifty francs apiece.

○

Kilometer 104–106. Camprieu. And back out of Camprieu – there's the hundred-meter downhill stretch I've been longing for for the last forty-five minutes. Been racing for three and a half hours, one to go; Kléber and Krabbé up front.

'Easy now,' Kléber hisses. Aha, that's a relief; I ease off a little. I take a slug of water and stuff a few slices of orange in my mouth. And a fig. Straight ahead of us is a darkness where Mont Aigoual must be.

We take turns pulling; now he hisses: '*Onafaydoumaynahj.*'

I look back, see Reilhan, no Lebusque. Reilhan hasn't cracked: he's a hundred meters behind us, he's trying to come back. Is this the decisive moment? On paper, Reilhan sprints better than I do. Should I give it everything I've got now, to lose him once and for all, and risk having Kléber dump me on Mont Aigoual?

I slow, Kléber takes over, Reilhan comes alongside. But Lebusque has been dropped – always the same old song and dance. Lebusque rides himself right out of the race. If he'd stayed with us to the Col de Perjuret, his downhill skills could have made him dangerous; those last eleven kilometers into Meyrueis are pretty much one long descent.

It's raining. We're on a wide stretch now, the only flat bit in the surroundings. Fields, campgrounds, handbills pointing out holiday fun. Skiing, the most beautiful grottoes.

A cow. It's not watching.

Kilometer 106–108. A fork in the road and a gendarme holding up a truck. He points to the left. Roux goes left, we have to go left too. There is a smaller road, going into the woods. It goes up, up there.

Climbing. Hands on the bars, my wrists in front of me. They're wet. Mont Aigoual is almost the highest mountain in the Cévennes, but height doesn't mean everything: in Holland there are hills steeper than Mont Ventoux. Mont Aigoual is tough, but regular. It's made up of three parts. First, three kilometers to the Col de la Sereyrède, then three kilometers to the ski area at the Col de Pra Peirot, then two more to the summit of Mont Aigoual itself.

Onafaydoumaynahj: On a fait du ménage! 'We did a little cleaning!' Hey, Reilhan, you know what Kléber just said? That we did a little cleaning. Meaning you!

But still, he *had* been dropped, Reilhan.

Forty-three nineteen. Krabbé's twenty was clean as a whistle. All Krabbé's sprockets were clean as a whistle, because it was raining. I drop back so Stéphan can pull up next to me. He rolls down his window and hands me a peeled banana, in two installments.

'It's going well,' he says calmly. A Tour de France rider peeling a banana for me: I would never have figured that on July 20, 1972.

Roux's car interrupts its music to tell a group of people, who are hunting for mushrooms at least fifty meters from the road, that Holland is a flat country but that it nonetheless produced a climber of Krabbé's caliber.

Tour de France, 1958. A few days before I saw Charly Gaul ride into the Parc des Princes in his yellow jersey, something new was introduced to the Tour: a 21.5-kilometer uphill time trial on Mont Ventoux.

I've cycled up Mont Ventoux on seven occasions. There are two routes you can choose from: one from the village of Malaucène, the other from Bédoin. They both last 21.5 kilometers, are both just as hard and just as sweet, and the last six kilometers of both pass through the famous moonscape. Simpson.

I always take the Bédoin side. The first five kilometers roll up slowly. There you're cycling away from the summit, which you can see over your left shoulder, a pastel-yellow wasteland with a dot on it: the Observatory. During the first few kilometers, Mont Ventoux doesn't so much give the impression of height as of pedestrian calm. You pass a little village of grayish-white houses where no one ever seems to notice people on bikes, and then you're in the forest.

The forest is the worst. For more than ten kilometers you climb along slopes of varying gradient, but always more than ten percent. A rhythm cannot be found. Standing on the pedals doesn't help, staying in the saddle doesn't help. Forty-three cannot be divided by twenty-two. Every thought immediately rolls out of the back of your head. Making good time doesn't work. You either make it or you don't: your watch just minds its own business.

Then, in some inexplicable fashion, you're actually out of the woods, you're at Chalet Reynard, a restaurant where the ski lifts start. There too begin the yellow barrens that last for another six kilometers. You ride a bit more easily there, because the Observatory, that eerie castle, keeps getting closer. Slogans are painted on the road: ALLEZ ALAIN SANTY. Every sixty seconds a cyclist comes shooting past on his way downhill, grinning at you. Fifteen hundred meters before the top, you pass the Simpson monument. This is where he suffocated in the heat in 1967, 'in a valiant attempt to win the Tour de France'. Let's not overdo it. The first time I saw the monument was on an April day when the mountainside was still covered in a meter and a half of snow. Only the tip of the stone was sticking out: you could see a rider's hunched back.

Every November Simpson is snowed under and spends the next five months frozen tight.

Whenever I come past him I say out loud: 'Hello, Tom.' In the 1970 Tour, Merckx doffed his cap here, even though the sun kept beating down and he was in a deep, black dip.

And then you're at the summit. You look out over the land; you drink a bit; a ruddy sense of well-being courses through your whole body, and a great desire wells up in you to climb this mountain again some day.

That I always choose the Bédoin side is not because of Simpson, but because that 1958 time trial began there as well. That way I can compare my times with those of the champions. Gaul came in first at 1 hour, 2 minutes and 9 seconds, which is still the record. He was taken from the summit to his hotel in an ambulance. Second was Bahamontes at 1.02.40; fifty-fifth, Wim van Est at 1.14.07.

There were ninety-five racers. The time limit was 1.22.52. Two riders didn't make that. They were taken out of the Tour and not allowed to start the next day. Too harsh for my taste. Any excuse to throw a rider out of a race is OK by me, but not that kind of inborn lack of athletic skill. That's not what road racing is about.

With my best time, I would have been the last of the non-eliminated riders. Ladies and gentlemen, please note in your programs: 92. Krabbé, 1.21.50.

Kilometer 108. Six kilometers to climb to the top of Mont Aigoual. A sign: CEVENNES NATIONAL PARK. BE CAREFUL

WITH FIRE. Further, higher, colder. My chest and cheeks are glowing, though, and my legs are red as brick. I think: 'Tonight I'll write in my logbook: "Aigoual climb went in a rush, didn't even feel the pedals", but tonight I won't be feeling what I'm feeling now.'

Only when I've given it fifty full strokes will I have given a stroke for every rider behind me! I'm climbing in a daze.

Have to piss.

Kilometer 108–109. And why should Kléber always be the one to lead the race? I move my wheel up half a meter, just past his. He doesn't like that, and snatches back a few centimeters. Then it's me again; a power struggle that could be won immediately by stepping out of one's role: well, Stani, if riding lead means so much to you . . . Oh no, I thought . . .

I leave him to it. Kléber leads the Tour de Mont Aigoual.

Kilometer 109. Col de la Sereyrède. An opening in the woods. A guardrail, a bench, a half a millstone, undoubtedly point-ing out the highlights of a panorama spreading for miles around. Mist.

To the right is a road down; to the left is one going up. A gendarme is pointing left. We go left.

Was that really the Col de la Sereyrède? That went quickly. Form.

Kilometer 110–111. The woods have closed again. Three contestants left, the race has entered its final hour. Kléber riding lead. Four more kilometers to the top of Mont Aigoual.

Suddenly I know that I'm going to attack. The decision catches me off guard. The way you can mull endlessly over getting up in the morning – and suddenly find yourself standing next to the bed. Your body got up, and you were in it.

But I'm allowed to choose the moment of my attack. When my second hand passes sixty. It's at fifty now. OK, then the next time. Ridiculous. This time. Seven seconds to go.

A great moment. I've been living for this race for so long, and these are the last few seconds before I break it wide open. Now that my decision's been made, I can explain it too: Reilhan is the only one who can still beat me. At Camprieu he showed that he was vulnerable. So I have to attack him.

Three more seconds. Entire worlds can be thought in three seconds.

Now.

My sporting career: 1954
Close to our house was a school with a little square in front of it: that's where we played soccer. Goals had been drawn on the walls of the school, with the names of clubs between the posts – 'Ajax', 'Blauw Wit' – and in one of the goals was written the name of the keeper of the Dutch national team: Kraak.

What a boring custom, I thought. So I took twenty pieces of chalk home from my own school, and early one Sunday morning I wrote in big fat letters on the wall: KRABBÉ. I drew my own goal around it.

That afternoon the new goal was broken in, and I boxed all the balls right out of it. A couple of boys acted like they were going to make fun of me, and I could understand that, but on the other hand: why should you have to achieve anything *before* being allowed to enjoy the glory? An eleven-year-old boy got a lot more enjoyment out of glory than a grown-up, but a boy that age hadn't had the chance to come up with the achievements. Was it really so terrible to switch the order around?

But what I had done was forbidden. And because the perpetrator of such crimes is usually located quite readily, that Monday morning the janitor of the school knocked on our door. My parents told me about it that evening. I had besmeared the walls of the school.

Besmeared!

I was given a bucket of water and a scrub brush, and I wiped out my name. From back to front. When only the first two letters were left, my identity seemed obliterated enough and I went home. And, indeed, I never heard another word about it.

Kilometer 111. Betrayal. 'That this Krabbé still has the energy for that kind of thing.' 'Co-operation is the only thing that can save us now.' 'Nothing can save us now.'

I'm gone, I shift, I lean on it, this is the jump you can

103

always make, the pain is a march by protesters who've forgotten to paint their signs.

But now everything is black. The woods are soundless and black. I drop back onto the saddle and hammer away. 'Hoo!! Hoo!!' I yell. The wisp of daze is gone from my kicks.

A flash over the shoulder. No one's on my wheel. I did it. I really did it. I've given the Tour de Mont Aigoual its final decisive twist.

I ease up a little and shift back to the nineteen. Up on the pedals one more time, back in the saddle. 'OoOo!! OoOo!!' There's something struggling in my head, trying to punch my eyeballs out from the inside. 'Hooob!' Let Roux get an earful of that, I'm in the process of recovery *during* effort, and this is how it goes. A flash over the shoulder, now I see Kléber at least a hundred meters behind me. I hawk, spit out a raindrop and slime. If I'm still alone when I get to the top of the Aigoual, I win.

Kilometer 111–112. A cold, wet forest is growing up around me. Mist, fog, no one. More than three and a half hours of racing.

And now don't look back any more. Ride!

Kilometer 112. Col de Pra Peirot. Suddenly a building in the mist beside the road. Black beams curve from ceiling to ground. This is where the ski lifts end. Are there people sitting in there, warm, looking at me? I picture them. I can't see more than fifty meters out in front, fuzzy red lights I can barely make out. Roux. I'm riding into a cloud.

From out of the mist, Kléber pops up beside me. My attack was designed to bring the two training buddies together in the lead. Everything's going the way it should. I can do anything now. Together we'll ride the rest of the way to Meyrueis. He'll help me hold the lead, and I win the sprint.

Kléber is gasping hard. I don't want to hear it. I don't want to fight against people with weaknesses, because it could always turn out that they were actually weaker than I was and that I should therefore have won. I only want to fight against pawns on bicycles. I want to be the one who *should* have lost, and then win. Kléber's gasping ought to remain tucked deep under his number.

Kilometer 113. Fog. I know we're out of the woods. These are the final, bare slopes of Mont Aigoual. Kléber waited his turn, but now he takes over. He's not pushing it as hard as I was, but I can use a breather.

Another half a kilometer to the top. We see nothing. An icy wind is blowing against my cheeks, unspoiled by journalism, ski lifts or even Tours de France – precisely as it was here a hundred thousand years ago, ready to serve as the décor for my victory.

LITTLE ABC OF ROAD RACING

ANQUETIL, JACQUES With him I once trained in the Olympic Stadium in Amsterdam. That was many years ago now.

Anquetil was waiting in the dressing room: you weren't allowed to start training until ten o'clock, and it wasn't ten yet. I said: 'Imagine that you went out onto the track too early. Then tomorrow's paper would say: "Anquetil Ten Seconds Too Early".' My belly shook with laughter at this, and Anquetil also found it highly amusing.

Then it was time. We swept through the curves like madmen. They'd hung a big second hand on the scoreboard, to make it easier to time your laps. After a while I realized that my bicycle had turned into a huge tablespoon. It was uncomfortable to ride, and hard to steer in the curves. But you should have seen it go! I was doing five-second laps.

COPPI, FAUSTO On his wheel I once climbed Mont Ventoux. He sat up the whole way, his long back straight as a ramrod. I had a book with me, and I held it against his back. It fit perfectly. That way I could profit most from Coppi's slipstream. So this was what they meant by 'sitting on a wheel'.

DONNER, HEIN A chess player, originally. Yet also a competent cyclist. Once I was in the same race with him. He rode lead, powerfully, his hands up on the bars. Quiet strokes of the pedal, calm authority. Escaping was out of the question. Donner felt a bit ridiculous in his racing outfit, but he realized there was no way around it. He had resigned himself to it.

KLÉBER, STANISLAS French bicycle racer. We once went in search of a treasure on the mountain where he always trained. Two men asked us for directions. I was about to tell them, but Kléber stopped me just in time. But on the mountain itself we ran into the same men, and a terrible fight ensued. We won. Then Kléber found the treasure. It was a tiny, grubby little chest, with some dirt and a few earrings in it. I was very disappointed, but Kléber said: 'It was only a minor treasure anyway.' Then I understood that it was wrong of me to have expected more.

After that we went to the hospital to have ourselves bandaged.

KRABBÉ, TIM Incredible *tour de force* during the 1973 Milan–San Remo. This previously unknown rider actually broke the World Hour Record *before* the start, and then went on to wrest a promising position in the race itself. On the final climb he made a solo attack to lead. During the descent his bicycle turned into a huge pillow, which nonetheless made it possible for him to sail through the curves with even greater ease. Nothing seemed to stand between him and a glorious victory! But alas! shortly before the finish he shot out of a curve, flew straight through two doors and landed in a huge beach-side restaurant, having received quite a blow to the head. Yet not all was lost, for it turned out that one of the restaurant corridors led to the finish as well. In a final desperate attempt, Krabbé spurred his pillow wildly down the corridor, bumping aside waiters with trays; he wanted to win so badly! But this final chance was ruined as well when the race director stopped him and gave him a terrible scolding. What made a novice like Krabbé think he could just go and win a classic, out in front of all those cracks?

Krabbé didn't know what to say. He realized that he had gone too far. One could not simply fly in the face of the established order in road racing. After having admitted to this, Krabbé collapsed completely. He was carried to the hospital through a side entrance. The next day the papers said: 'He was shaking like a leaf.'

KUIPER, HENNIE My rival during the finals of a major sporting tournament for bicycle racers. The preliminaries consisted of skating contests. All events were won by Nils Aaness, a skater himself, so the results didn't count. The great champion of the tournament was 'the Norwegian, God'. During the semifinals, however, God was trounced by Kuiper, and I won from the chess player Hans Ree. Our event consisted of throwing tennis balls into each other's goals. During our match, Ree was disqualified 'because he had deflected the ball from under the crossbar'. I thought that was a ridiculous reason for disqualifying someone, but I kept my mouth shut.

During the finals I blocked everything Kuiper threw my way, and I threw all mine in. 50–0! The champ!

LEBUSQUE I once went out for an evening with the Lebusques. We had agreed to meet in the station restaurant. We were barely seated when Lebusque insisted on a test of strength: a little arm-wrestling. I was able to get out of this by saying that I already knew he was stronger than me. Lebusque then began eating his glass. He chomped on the shards. I considered this a banal display of sturdy teeth, far beneath his dignity, and told him so. Besides, I was afraid he would cut himself. 'It's much more clever, for example, to let salt come pouring out of your hand, for half an hour or so,' I said.

'Aha!' Lebusque said. 'That is the most spectacular trick of the famous magician Fred Kaps. We are great admirers of his.' And he and his wife began talking excitedly about a Fred Kaps show they had once attended.

MERCKX, EDDY Once asked to borrow my fork. I was riding in a long and tough race, I had escaped from the peloton and was soloing out in front. The road consisted of a layer of fried mashed potatoes, which my mother had gone to the trouble to prepare. I had a fork with me, and used it to take bites from the ground as I rode. Merckx caught up with me. He was hungry too, and asked to borrow my fork.

PELLENAARS, KEES Watched me repair a tire after I'd had a puncture. I tore the old tube off the rim, smeared the rim with glue and stuck the new tire to it. At least, that's what I thought, but I had glued the old tube back in place! I asked Pellenaars whether this had ever happened to him. First he tried to deny it, but then he started laughing and confessed. Yes, he too had had this happen to him.

REILHAN, ROGER Together we escaped during a trying race. Gale-force wind in our faces, rain. But we worked together well and steadily increased our lead. The road was a broad mat that wasn't stitched down well at the sides. We were able to grab the loose edges with our hands and in that way pull ourselves along. Good thing too, because, besides having the wind in our faces, we also seemed to be glued to the ground.

There were a lot of people watching along the road. I could feel them thinking: 'Yes, a bicycle racer needs strong arms as well. But that Krabbé's got 'em.'

We received reports that a group of very serious opponents were on our tail. Merckx, Verbeeck, De Vlaeminck, Thurau, Barthélemy. 'We really have to push on now,' I said to Reilhan, 'otherwise they'll catch us.'

Suddenly I had a good idea: I'd tell him I had a diamond in my mouth. Of course he wouldn't believe it, but after the race he would tell all the other riders and they would realize that I was extremely talented and brilliant, because of the bravura with which I tried to trick someone into thinking something like that.

I was riding lead, and I turned around: 'Hey, Reilhan, take a good look between my lips. I've got a diamond in my mouth, see?'

He looked and said no. My plan was failing! He actually did believe that I had a diamond in my mouth, he thought he just couldn't see it.

'Reilhan, take a good look now. I really have a diamond in my mouth.'

'Well, I don't see anything.'

We were indeed overtaken by Merckx and the others. They had a Russian with them now. The course ran through a movie theater, where I fell behind because I stopped to shake hands with everyone.

So I went to the finish line as a spectator instead. During the final descent, the Russian had a fatal accident. Merckx won, which was fairly easy for him because Thurau had a pistol and was holding Verbeeck and De Vlaeminck at gunpoint. So ended a race which I, had I not made that stupid mistake in the movie theater, could just as well have won myself!

Kilometer 114. A strange, broad stretch. A parking lot for skiers. They ski here until April. No one. I can't see the sides of the road. The rustle of a bike . . . I look around: Reilhan.

Fucking hell.

Now I should go right away again – *I've* recovered and *he's* ridden his guts out. A line, the summit of the Mont Aigoual.

Too late.

○

Kilometer 114–118. Someone is standing and shivering next to his car, and shouts cheerfully: 'All downhill from here!' He points to a gray mass below us.

Now I'm descending, so I have to stop cycling. So I have to start freezing. The cold skips all kinds of phases, it's in my bones right away. My hands! My handlebars are an operating table where the cutting is done without anaesthetic. I make my legs go round and round, frontwards, backwards, but there's nothing to expend energy on. Can't work up body heat to protect me now. My sweat freezes. The rain freezes on my forehead.

I shout: 'Hoom! Hoom!' The wind cuts right through my undershirt. I don't have a newspaper under it. At the top of every mountain, Bahamontes stuffed a newspaper under his jersey. As soon as he finished his ice-cream cone, he stuffed a newspaper under his jersey.

So now I'm crying out loud.

That time in April when I climbed past the walls of ice on the Ventoux, I never suspected that the real hardship would come during the descent. Halfway down through the snowy moonscape I was able to use the only unfrozen muscle I had left to brake, and climbed off. I walked until my blood started flowing again, but after I'd been rolling downhill a bit my forehead and hands began to freeze, and I had to walk again. When I got to Bédoin it turned out that I had descended from the Ventoux a full three minutes faster than Gaul had climbed it.

In interviews with riders that I've read and in conversations I've had with them, the same thing always comes up: the best part was the suffering. In Amsterdam I once trained with a Canadian rider who was living in Holland. A notorious creampuff: in the sterile art of track racing he was Canadian champion in at least six disciplines, but when it came to toughing it out on the road he didn't have the character.

The sky turned black, the water in the ditch rippled, a heavy storm broke loose. The Canadian sat up straight, raised his arms to heaven and shouted: 'Rain! Soak me! Ooh, rain, soak me, make me wet!'

How can that be: suffering is suffering, isn't it?

In 1910, Milan–San Remo was won by a rider who spent half an hour in a mountain hut, hiding from a snowstorm. Man, did he suffer!

In 1919, Brussels–Amiens was won by a rider who rode the last forty kilometers with a flat front tire. Talk about suffering! He arrived at 11.30 at night, with a ninety-minute lead on the only other two riders who finished the race. That day had been like night, trees had whipped back and forth, farmers were blown back into their barns, there were hailstones, bomb craters from the war, crossroads where the gendarmes had run away and riders had to climb onto one another's shoulders to wipe clean the muddied road signs.

Oh, to have been a rider then. Because after the finish all the suffering turns to memories of pleasure, and the greater the suffering, the greater the pleasure. That is Nature's payback to riders for the homage they pay her by suffering. Velvet pillows, safari parks, sunglasses: people have become woolly mice. They still have bodies that can walk for five days and four nights through a desert of snow, without food, but they accept praise for having taken a one-hour bicycle ride. 'Good for you.' Instead of expressing their gratitude for the rain by getting wet, people walk around with umbrellas. Nature is an old lady with few suitors these days, and those who wish to make use of her charms she rewards passionately.

That's why there are riders.

Suffering you need; literature is baloney.

If ever there was a Rider of the Apocalypse, it was Gaul. When we last saw him, an ambulance had just dropped him at his hotel after a time trial up the Ventoux in 1958. He had pushed himself hard, because it was hot that day and he hated the heat. The next day of that Tour he lost twelve minutes; the day after that, a few more, because it was still hot. Gaul was more than fifteen minutes behind the yellow jersey, he was done for. Then came the twenty-first stage, through the Alps. Hail, black skies, storms, the end of the world from morning to night.

Far out in front of all the other riders was Gaul. The wind flogged him, the rain lashed down on him, and he took back his fifteen minutes and won the Tour.

Giro d'Italia, 1956. With two more stages to go, Gaul was around sixteenth in the standings, more than twenty minutes behind the leader. Next-to-last stage: Merano–Trento, 242 kilometers through the Dolomites.

Of the eighty-seven riders who started that day, forty-six abandoned the race. According to Daan de Groot, one of the heroes who completed the stage, an even better indication of the day's horrors was that Pellenaars had advised him to go into a restaurant and warm up a little. Pellenaars, who would rather see his riders dead than alive in the sag car! Pellenaars, talking about warming up a little!

The frost penetrated deep into the reporters' microphones; it hailed, it rained, it snowed. There was no place that day for those vulnerable, shelter-dependent cables we call muscles. Jan Nolten was shivering so badly he couldn't steer any more, and had to abandon. He was too skinny for that stage. Wout Wagtmans got off at a café and put both feet, complete with shoes, in a bucket of hot water. Fornara, wearing the leader's jersey, stuck it out for 240 kilometers but couldn't possibly finish those last two, and abandoned. For Schoenmakers, the suffering didn't instantly turn into memories of pleasure at the finish line; he had gone blind, and screamed that he would never see again. Anyone climbing off to pull on a pair of training pants was frozen to the road until long after the time limit. Anyone taking a piss was immediately bolted to the ground by a yellow parabola. No one pissed. The sag car had to abandon. The riders descended inch by inch, squeezing their brakes so they could still spin their pedals. Ambulances with shrieking sirens drove back and forth, lightning crackled, it was dark as night; in a word, the weather was awful.

The last sixteen kilometers had to be climbed up a mountain completely blocked by snow. Soldiers with brooms cleared a path for the riders and pushed them up. Daan de Groot went up like a bucket of water to a medieval fire. 'I didn't have to pedal once.' There were no race officials anywhere. 'It was a huge mess. They were glad to have any results at all.'

Half a snowstorm before the others, Gaul reached the top of that mountain. Here I have a photograph, taken about an hour before Daan de Groot came in. Gaul never got a push uphill. He'd screamed and begged for it, but, stupidly enough, in French. The soldiers preferred to see an Italian come in before anyone who begged for help in French. In my photograph, Gaul's little body is hanging, more or less unconscious, in the arms of two policemen. The most amazing thing about it is that, where the two men are holding his thighs, the flesh actually gives.

Gaul had won the Giro d'Italia.

I think Gaul suffered the same way others did, but he enjoyed it more. That's of course also why he was such a good climber. Maybe he was only happy when feeling pain; maybe he came from a line that had lived more slowly and stood closer to the forces of nature.

I paid a visit to Gaul's former *soigneur*, Gerrit Visser, to find out how that worked.

'Did Gaul ride so well in bad weather because he liked to suffer?'

'Well . . . during bad weather, a lot of oxygen is released.'

'But lightning and hail, for example, didn't that perk him up?'

'Of course! Because he was able to assimilate a huge amount of oxygen.'

'Sure, of course. But wasn't he a person who went looking for punishment?'

'Yes . . . but oxygen really played a major role. Oxygen! You see, Gaul was able to assimilate more oxygen than most people, so when the weather was bad . . .'

'But didn't you ever have the impression that rain and hail and that kind of thing gave him a sort of energy?'

'Absolutely! Because then there was more oxygen in the air!'

Gaul couldn't do without pain: pain was his motor. It's a mistake to leave it up to the facts to tell themselves.

In every report from 1967, you'll see that Simpson's heart broke three kilometers from the top of the Ventoux. The monument honoring his death is located one and a half kilometers from the top. Rightly so. More tragic. The facts miss the heart of the matter; to give us a clear picture, the facts need a vehicle, the anecdote.

When Geldermans told me that Anquetil always moved his water bottle to his back pocket during climbs, so his bike would be lighter, I began paying attention. I noticed that in all the old pictures of Anquetil climbing, his bidon is always in its holder. That's straining at gnats. Geldermans' story strikes to the soul of the rider, and is therefore true.

Those pictures are inaccurate.

Kilometers 118–120. Pain. And what about it?

Whatever the case, this is an easy descent. Broad roads, not too curvy, not too steep.

We pass through a village: Cabrillac. Five jettisoned cobblestones, three houses. Is it still raining? Probably, but the question does arise, and that's something.

For the first time since the Aigoual, I'm allowed to ride

again. With a *faux plat* going up, I cycle in a gear that's way too low, to spin myself warm. And down again, and up again. The other two are still Kléber and Reilhan. We leave the mist, we've come down out of a cloud. We, the only three left in this backbreaker of a race. We have to stay together. More than once, the Eleven Cities Tour, the grueling 200-kilometer skating race in Holland that can only be held every ten years or so, has ended with a bunch of skaters crossing the finish together in first place, arms around one another's shoulders. Of course, solidarity was another great excuse not to bear the uncertainties and pain of the individual attempt, but nevertheless and foremost: those skaters had grown to love each other too much to battle it out in a final sprint.

It's not raining here, or at least in far fewer drops. Do they really expect me to sprint later on, with these stiff legs?

It's not raining any more. Thank God, another uphill bit. I'm riding lead. I have to work to get dry. We've even got a landscape here, the final plateau. To the right, woods, to the left, wide, shimmery fields of Van Gogh-yellow, in the upper left-hand corner a watery yellow blur. Far from here there must be cracks in the landscape where our former racing companions might still be slogging away.

Another eighteen kilometers; not much. Should I really sprint against Reilhan? I have no idea where I could lose him. And if I sprint, is it better to shift one last time before the finish, or isn't it?

It was stupid of me to let Kléber take over on the Aigoual.

If you want to blow a real gap, you have to do it on your own.

Should I attack? I don't dare.

Been racing for more than four hours; less than half an hour to go. Kléber does dare to attack. I can't believe my eyes. A little warning tinkle and off he goes. I can barely believe it, he's outdoing himself today. I keep taking my pull, then look back. Reilhan doesn't take his. I drop back, and we ride on beside each other in amazement and silence. This is really going too far. If Reilhan thinks *I'm* going to bridge that gap for *him*, the better sprinter, he's got another thing coming.

Nothing happens. Kléber looks back and increases his lead.

'Hey, Reilhan.'

He looks at me.

'Ho hey.'

I'm getting drier by the minute.

Kléber leaves us even further behind.

'Hell, Reilhan, it's up to you, but as far as I'm concerned Kléber wins this one.'

'Oh, fine by me.'

The theme of mutual self-destruction, once again. A beloved theme in bicycle racing; more races are lost than won. Questions arise. How badly does Reilhan want to win? How badly does he think I want to win? How much does he think I like the idea of Kléber winning? How much do I like the idea of Kléber winning? How much does Reilhan like the idea of me losing? How far can we let Kléber go before he becomes unstoppable?

Reilhan jumps, I hop his wheel, he stops pedaling, I barrel past him, he hops my wheel, I stop pedaling.

We pant, Kléber rides away from us. Further and further away he is, he looks back a few times, full of disbelief. He's never won a race in his life. I'm his friend. After we'd known each other for four years, he showed me a cigar box full of index cards, with his times on his pet mountain calligraphed on them. Date, average speed, gear used, comments. His favorite opponent is himself. He's unbending. Above a certain limit, his times lose the right to go in the cigar box.

I sense that I'm the only one to whom he's ever shown that cigar box. Just because he always rides so conscientiously against me in races, does that mean I have to race against *him* this time? Suddenly it dawns on me: this is my chance to take the final, most distinguished step in the hierarchy of road racing: from winning to letting win. A huge emptiness unfolds in me. I lay my hands on the bars and sit up. Reilhan sits up. Either he takes me there or we'll sprint for second place, a sprint that I, with a great show of disdain, will let him win.

Another example.

Tour de France, 1977. During the decisive stage, Van Impe made his escape and, at a given point, had such a huge lead that it seemed the Tour was in his pocket.

Behind him, three riders had come together: Thévenet (in the yellow jersey), Kuiper and Zoetemelk, the only other riders who still had a chance. Thévenet was riding lead; the two Dutchmen were refusing to help. Kuiper planned to lick Thévenet's plate clean before starting on his own. If at that point Thévenet had done what his team manager advised him to do, namely allow the two Dutchmen to hang themselves with their own rope, he would have hanged with them and all three would have lost the Tour.

But Thévenet shouldered the blackmailing of the yellow jersey and of his ambition, and pulled the lead for the others. As was to be expected, Kuiper and Zoetemelk profited from this by escaping from Thévenet's wake on the last mountain. Zoetemelk cracked, but Kuiper passed Van Impe, who was badly cracked as well, and won the stage. But not the yellow jersey; in a fantastic comeback, during which he forced things harder than he had ever forced them in his career, Thévenet was able to keep the damage precisely within bounds and kept the yellow jersey all the way to Paris.

His scheme had failed, but what Kuiper did was coolly calculating, tactically perfect and constituted his best shot at winning the Tour de France. But it also sprang from a less generous heart than he's usually given credit for. Because, at the level of a Kuiper or a Thévenet, the sport is exclusively about honor. And no matter how Kuiper had advanced his chances of winning the Tour by hanging on Thévenet's wheel, he had destroyed every chance of winning the Tour *grandly*.

Thévenet won it grandly.

Kilometer 120. Unbelievable, but Reilhan persists in his refusal. Why doesn't his father come along and explain to him what a shameless display this is? Or does he actually teach his son to race like this?

But I can't do this.

I've dreamed too much of winning this race. I can't do it, just let the victory pedal away from me. My dreams are worth more than Reilhan's. It's not the one with the best chances who's open to blackmail, but the one with the strongest will. Me!

If I wait for just one more second, Reilhan may lose his patience, but I don't even want that any more. I'm going to show him how one goes about racing on a bicycle. Not small, but grand. I'll rob my friend of the victory, I'll take the best sprinter up to the lead, but at least, before his father's eyes, I'll make him show himself for what he is: a wheel-sucker.

My sporting career: 1954

MINISTRY OF SOCIAL AFFAIRS
Department of Vocational Information
Amsterdam, Nieuwe Doelenstraat 6–8
Name and address: *Tim Krabbé, Amstelkade 12hs, A'dam*
Date of birth: 4.13.1943
Date of examination: 3.25.1954

RECOMMENDATION:
There is no doubt that Tim has the capacities needed
to attend secondary school. Intelligence and self-sufficiency
are both at the requisite level. This self-sufficiency
expresses itself in the desire to find his own way, and in
a reticence to accept help. Tim is not particularly
childish, and any lack of knowledge is one he can
compensate for at secondary school by means of his facile
and penetrating powers of comprehension. Because he is
quite solitary and ambitious, we would recommend
sending Tim to a Dalton school. It would be very good
for this little boy if the definitive choice between
secondary schools could be postponed for a few years.
Tim is excellently suited to be a professional bicycle racer.

Kilometer 121. 'Hey, Reilhan.'
   He's acting like he doesn't hear me.
   'I've got a deal for you.'
   Now he's looking at me.
   'Today you win the wheel–sucker race, and I win the real
race. OK?'
   He doesn't even blink. I turn back, I tighten my grip, I'm
going to bridge that gap.
   A bang, my front rim rattles over the ground. I brake and
climb off. Reilhan sprints away. Reilhan's father drives past. I
try to loosen the wheel, but the division of my hand into
fingers is a useless fluke of Nature now. I just stand there
slamming my palm against the quick–release until Stéphan
comes rushing up. He whips the wheel out of the fork, puts

in a new one, helps me onto my bike, pushes me rolling again, and as he does he's given me one quick order, which is: 'Win!'

Kilometer 121–123. I pedal. I'm once again able to translate my situation into terms I can understand: all is lost. I may be cycling again now, but what I want doesn't make it to my wheels. I give it everything, but of course Reilhan is doing the same and that makes him go faster than I do. He widens his lead, then disappears from sight. Maybe he's already caught up with Kléber. He won't even look to see whether Kléber can stay on his wheel, he'll ride straight on to Meyrueis, and if Kléber is still with him there he'll beat him in the sprint, as sure as two is greater than one.

I can't do it any more. I really can't do it any more. Getting off the bike like that has destroyed everything. Up to and including Koblet, riders had to strip off their own punctures, put on the new tubes and pump them up, before bridging the gap. Tiemen Groen's cotter pin came loose: he climbed off, borrowed a hammer from a farmer, knocked it in snugly again, climbed back on and won by a minute and a half. I can't do it any more. Someone else wins the Tour de Mont Aigoual.

Honking and shouting, there's Stéphan, pulling up beside me. Rolls down his window, sits there screaming. 'Uusk, uusk,' he's shouting. Probably wants me to go faster. Precisely what I can't do. He's fond of me, I rode my first race with him, in his races I've grown to become something of a rider, for his club I've won races, I'm his very own *vedette*. But, my good Stéphan, I'm only giving it everything I've got because no one says I have to. Only when there are arguments *for* something can there be arguments *against* it. The only times I've ever abandoned a race for lack of morale were when someone had gone with me specially to watch.

'Uuusk!'

Everything hurts. No matter how hard I breathe, I can't suck a void in the air that Reilhan will come tumbling into backwards. No, I can't do it any more now. That's right. I'm not even supposed to be able to do it any more. Truly excel, that's what other people do.

That road racing of mine, that was only a joke, of course. Maybe it did go a little too far: five thousand hours of training and three hundred and nine races, just to play the cyclist.

It was wonderful, though, that having started at the age of thirty I was still able to get a body that could really do something, that came in a solid twelfth in races amid a hundred hungry twenty-one-year-olds, that won occasionally in lesser races, that won regularly with Stéphan. It was wonderful enough to have taught any number of these glory boys a lesson in strength, in courage, in character. But a major road race is something I've never won. And therefore I also won't win the sweetest, the toughest of them all, the Tour de Mont Aigoual.

That's right.

I admit that that's right.

A final raindrop blows by, the spray of bike tires on the wet road, and a man in the yellow and blue of a tropical bird rides past me.

Kilometer 123–125. Lebusque.

Forty-two years of age, that guy. I know him. There he goes, past me, going faster than I can.

He growls, he waggles his eyebrows, he nods: come on. I wish people would just leave me alone. I come up out of the saddle and don't drop back down right away, at least that's something.

I wring my way onto his wheel. My legs feel like the rope in the finals of the World Championship Tug of War. Now *I'm* going faster than I can, too. Jesus Christ, that Lebusque.

My pull, not a chance. I'm dying on his wheel. Everything tells me I won't be able to stick with him, but since July 20, 1972, pain is no longer a signal to stop. Krabbé was towed to the finish in an easy chair.

The last few kilometers before the Col de Perjuret. No landscape here. Here there's only Lebusque's back wheel. How am I ever going to get rid of this guy? If only I'd come down with a puncture. How often, fighting away in a long-beaten peloton that nonetheless lay down a hellish tempo I could barely follow, have I longed for a flat tire? A puncture, permission from beyond to stop the dying.

For years, something kept me from talking to other riders about that longing, but when I did it turned out they all knew the feeling. A lot of praying goes on in the peloton, especially to God and to Linda. Please let me get a puncture. But the speed of prayer has its limits, so the rider occasionally resorts to more drastic measures. He pounds his wheels through potholes, through gravel, searches for sharp rocks and, perchance, when he has a race to ride but no morale, he'll even mount a carefully selected tube that's ready to blow.

There are riders with glasses who treat rain as a puncture. Punctures take the weirdest forms. Some riders who have to do without glasses consider a snapped brake cable to be a puncture, or the witnessing of more than two crashes. At the start of Race 129 (July 28, 1974) in the town of Hoogkarspel, my first race of more than a hundred kilometers, I was extremely tense. There were a multitude of signs that something terrible was about to happen, but not a single excuse not to start. Criteriums in Holland! Curve, sprint, brake, curve, sprint, brake, curve, sprint, brake, curve, every twenty seconds a curve, a hard-riding house of pain, two-and-a-half hours long, unimaginable if you've never been in it yourself. But even though I tagged along quite well in the peloton, the tension didn't go away. After forty kilometers, one of my front spokes popped. It didn't fall out, it just rattled along. There didn't seem to be any problem – the wheel didn't rub, there was barely a wobble to it. I wondered whether here one could speak of a puncture. The spoke could come flying out any moment, and then my puncture would be gone. I climbed off. Puncture. In my cycling logbook, under 'results', I wrote: *malfunction*.

But when no heed is given to your longing for a puncture, there's nothing left but to suffer. Suffering is an art. Like the downhills, it's a non-athletic art in which the great champions nevertheless outstrip all amateurs. On all seven of my climbs of Mont Ventoux, I arrived at the top feeling fresh. Gaul had to take an ambulance to his hotel, and when

Merckx won there in 1970 he collapsed and had to be put in an oxygen tent. Jan Janssen: now there was a man who knew how to hit bottom! He'd sink his teeth into the wheel in front of him and grind until everything went black. He gnashed his way across the mountains, and sometimes after a stage he would fall, bicycle and all, against the crush barrier, unable to speak a word for the next ten minutes. Character. In 1970, during Paris–Tours, Jan Janssen succeeded in cycling himself a minor heart seizure. He had to go into the hospital: it was more or less the end of his career. Altig could hit bottom hard, Geldermans could do it, Simpson could do it too.

And sometimes the suffering ends with you getting dumped, but that's peanuts. That's something your body takes care of for you, you watch in amazement as it happens.

I crack. Lebusque looks back, slows, screams. What does this guy want from me, anyway? Now I'm back on his wheel. I'm a big duck with big flat feet that's having a hard time. I could tell Lebusque: if you don't dump me, I promise I won't sprint. But you can't offer someone a gift of third place. Besides, he doesn't want to dump me, that's what he just said.

Hey: are my brains making thoughts again? There's even a landscape here. It's no wider than the road but, still, it's there.

Kilometer 125–126. With each breath, Lebusque pulls the world a little closer. One more kilometer to the Col de Perjuret. The bottom of a *faux plat* going down, the start of a *faux plat* going up. More shutters fly open: we're riding through a forest of pine. Nice. The dirt beside the road is red. In the sky is an opening of blue.

Twelve more kilometers to race. The worst of my dip is leaving me. I go past Lebusque and take a pull. Now wait and see if he thinks I'm going fast enough. No. Stay on my wheel, he motions. OK, Lebusque.

We've left the woods, we're climbing through open space.

Now I see something that shocks me. Two hundred meters in front of me are Kléber and Reilhan. That's not what shocks me – Kléber is riding lead. I feel a cold shiver.

The *un*believable smallness.

The smallness, the blunder! Why would Kléber, who knows he's beaten anyway, contribute anything to Reilhan's speed? But Reilhan finds the idea of doing anyone even the slightest favor *so* intolerable, he can't see that. No. That's not what shocks me either.

I still have a chance to win the Tour de Mont Aigoual!

The final meters of the *faux plat*. Below us we see the crossroads at the Col de Perjuret. In the bareness around the fork in the road is a huge house with dark shutters closed. Kléber and Reilhan go left and start on the final descent into Meyrueis. Our lag has grown by meters, shrunk by seconds.

At the side of the road a little old lady is standing, dressed completely in black. Under her arm she holds a bundle of twigs. When she sees us, a smile of surprised recognition appears on her face. '*Allez, Bobet*,' she says.

I go past Lebusque.

The view here is complete. Spots of sunlight blow over the big Causse Méjean across from me. One of them blows right past me. Vapors rise from the crevices. Lebusque comes past me again. 'Ride,' he says.

Kilometer 126. Col de Perjuret, altitude 1,028 m. Another eleven kilometers to the finish. Been racing for four hours and twenty minutes: in a little more than a quarter of an hour, the outcome will be known.

We go left.

The champions have better bikes, more expensive shoes, many more pairs of cycling shorts than we do, but they have the same roads. On July 10, 1960, Roger Rivière came up this same road. Rivière was twenty-four years old, had already been World Pursuit Champion a few times, held the World Hour Record (despite a flat helium tire) and was the future winner of no fewer than four Tours de France. The 1960 Tour de France was going to be the first. He was already number two in the general classification, with a marginal lag behind Nencini, a normal champion, not a rider from a different planet, not like Rivière.

At the top of the Col de Perjuret, Rivière shifted down and began on the descent that would have been a right turn for Lebusque and me.

Where is the frame he rode on then? The Col de Perjuret is a meaningless col. Rivière descended on Nencini's wheel. He missed a curve, it's as simple as that. He tumbled headfirst over a wall and floated through the air.

A man's brains keep working while he's floating through the air. Rivière is floating there magnificently. All his responsibilities are behind him. Now it's up to powers greater than his to decide what's going to happen. He's on vacation, right in the middle of the Tour de France. But after a while his thoughts take on a more somber tone. Will, for example, his wheels be all right later on, when he lands? And, if not, how fast can his team director get him new ones? Maybe he'll hurt his knee when he comes down, and that will cause him problems during the rest of the race. Or maybe his chest will be cracked a little and they'll have to doctor him up before he can ride on. Or break a leg – then he'd have to abandon the Tour. But ah – useless, wearisome speculations. As long as you're flying like a bird you should make the most of it. And just like me, Rivière promises himself that, at the age of eighty, he'll have himself taken up as high as possible in a light plane and then jump out, without a parachute. Maybe make that eighty-one. As late as he can, but before the others do, as Henri Pélissier said.

Rivière fell fifteen meters. He landed in the bed of a little stream, covered in dead leaves. He remained lying there perfectly still, his back broken. Race officials and journalists came rushing down. One photographer felt that Rivière wasn't in the perfect position for a photo; he wanted to change something about it, but found himself obstructed by his professional ethics: the journalist's job is to record, not to intervene. So he said: 'Roger.' And Rivière, fully conscious but with a stabbing pain in his back, turned to him and looks at me. His head, on those dead ferns, is glistening with sweat, his right hand is tucked under his cheek, his left eye is open: it has seen everything from the change of a wheel up to and including death. They say that after his accident Rivière was as cheerful as ever. He never rode again, and died of cancer at forty. He was born for bad luck.

The Perjuret is a point of interest.

Kilometer 126–130. Left, I'm going down in front of Lebusque. Apparently Reilhan's father has received a signal from Roux; he drops back and we pass him.

Hairpin turns and ravines, the standard recipe. Gray of boulders, green of pastures. After every curve I sprint, until I have to brake again. I'm not having any trouble with these curves, I'm much too tired now to worry about matters of life and death. This is about something completely different: about me winning this race. On the shelf below I can already see Kléber. Without Reilhan. Two curves later I have Kléber on the straight stretch in front of me and Reilhan on the shelf below. Across the top of my head I feel a shiver coming up, like the copper comb on a fireman's helmet. I pass Kléber. On a longer, straighter stretch, Reilhan's in front of me. Now I miss having my thirteen. Hell with it. I'm not breathing any more either. I sprint dry, straight off the brains. I'm with Reilhan. This was Krabbé's unbelievable comeback. After 130 kilometers, with seven kilometers to go, Krabbé's spare front wheel is the first in the Tour de Mont Aigoual.

Kilometer 130–132. Lebusque and Kléber have joined us too; a four-man lead going into the final kilometers. Wind in the face, all that's left of the descent is a *faux plat.* Shreds of sunlight. The day is running down. Five-thirty. Lebusque attacks. Well, attack . . . he bobs past us like an old, rotten surfboard, he's already worked so hard today. Kléber goes to him, me, Reilhan. Four-man break. Ten more minutes to go.

If anyone really attacked now, I wouldn't be able to follow. Can they tell that by looking at me? I'm too exhausted to hide my exhaustion.

Lebusque has played his last card; that dawns on me only now. He had to use up his downhill skills to catch Reilhan. And what about me? I was too tired not to beat him to it.

Lebusque holds the lead. That makes it hard for anyone to attack: great. Although I wouldn't know which one of us would attack. Kléber? He never attacks. Reilhan? On paper he's the best sprinter, he'll wait for the sprint. When I think about that I can feel my throat fill with a yellow, soapy powder. But why? I know for a fact that when that sprint starts, everything in me will be perfectly still and certain.

Kilometer 132. A village: Salvensac. A few houses in the fields along the Jonte. Smoke. Five more kilometers to Meyrueis. Salvensac, filthy wine in a sack. An old man once lived here who mashed his grapes with dirty feet. Everyone thought his wine tasted filthy. Must have been three hundred years ago.

In ten minutes, the outcome will be known. Always the illusion that *somewhere* the future is already fixed, that you're just not allowed to know it yet. But you're riding into the void.

I look back. Maybe Reilhan's just stupid, maybe that's it. I tighten my toe-clips. For the sprint, Reilhan thinks. I attack. I drill into the wind, I give it everything; the pain leaps from a kilometer marker onto my back. I gargle, I spit. Completely everything, I have to win. Another twenty kicks, then I'm allowed to know what happened. I count the strokes of my right pedal, I can't do that with my left. Twenty, horrible. Zero.

I look back. Reilhan's sitting on my wheel. Kléber and Lebusque nowhere in sight, dumped.

Kilometer 133. Reilhan and I are the only ones left, the two strongest. I think, 'Now I'm completely and absolutely dead.' Reilhan jumps. I think, 'No, no,' but I hop his wheel. He looks back, stops pedaling. He was *hoping* I'd come along: Reilhan is as dead as I am. I pounce. He comes back. I stop pedaling. That was my last attack. I can't do it any closer to the end or I'll blow my sprint.

Reilhan and I: the last two.

Riding next to each other.

Kilometer 134. Incredible that I'm going to have to sprint with these stiff legs. 'A true sprinter can always sprint, even when he's dead.' The houses we're coming past now wouldn't be here if there were no Meyrueis. We ride side by side, not fast; we're keeping a quarter of an eye on each other.

Kilometer 135. A kilometer marker: MEYRUEIS 1.6. With that, this marker steps out of its role. It is the silent witness to our struggle, and should keep its banal little comments to itself. We peer around. Behind us, nothing. Three more minutes. Oh, how easy it will look on paper: '. . . and in the final sprint Krabbé soundly trounced the younger Reilhan by a length', but nothing in those words will show how much of my life went into this.

I still don't know whether I'm going to shift during the sprint. That doesn't bother me. That will take care of itself when the time comes. Right now I feel perfectly strong. I'm sitting wedged in like a spring between handlebars, saddle and pedals. Everything is forgotten. In my head it's quiet, sure and strong.

Reilhan looks at me. I look at him. We're riding beside each other. I almost find it hard not to smile: no one can take from us where we are right now.

Kilometer 136. The final kilometer. I peer around, he peers around, there's the sign saying MEYRUEIS. I look back; two hundred meters behind us are two sympathetic, hunched-over dots: Lebusque and Kléber. Too late for them.

Two men along the road look at us. 'My, those fellows are looking admirably fit. That's right, they're the leaders in the Tour de Mont Aigoual. After 150 kilometers, five or maybe even six cols, hail, mist, misery, they're all that's left of fifty-three men. I wish I was him, the older one.'

Two minutes from now the outcome of the Tour de Mont Aigoual will be known for ever. I already know the outcome, and at the same time I know: the future won't be outfoxed by anything, not even by my certainty.

Nonsense, says the expert, real certainty *makes* the future. I introduce him to my companion of the moment. 'Reilhan, *coureur cycliste*. Is every bit as certain that *he's* going to win. So what now? Shall we sprint for it?'

Whenever anyone beat the great Dutch sprinting champion Piet Moeskops on his weak point, he would promptly make sure he lost a few times in other ways: sprinting can be as convoluted as espionage. There are a thousand different sprints and a thousand kinds of sprinters. I'm the kind of sprinter who's doomed to being dumb, that's my strength. Here, my plan is being handed to me. I didn't have to think about it: a serene general went to a filing cabinet and took out a folder with a ready-made plan of attack, in the form of the monologue in which I later explain to Kléber how I won.

'You see, Stani, I'm pretty fast, but Reilhan is faster. Doesn't matter. We're *different* sprinters, that's what counts. I'm strong, I can ride faster and longer on a big gear than most people, but Reilhan has a real jump, his first push is a lot faster. A lot. Last week I made the mistake of letting him go first through the last curve. Then he was gone. He didn't keep it up, I almost caught him, but too late. This time I wasn't going to give him that chance. That's why I stayed in the lead through the curves, so I could take off right after the last one. You see, Stani, I accepted the disadvantage of having him on my wheel but I avoided the disadvantage of his jump, and that would have been worse. Road racing takes nerve.'

Fifty meters in front of me is my sign. CULTE PROTESTANTE. I tighten my toe clips. Slight sense of embarrassment. Reilhan tightens his toe clips. I tighten mine again. I shift down to the fifteen.

The sign. Four hundred meters to go. I speed up, I move out in front. To give Reilhan a scare, I come up out of the saddle. I get a scare myself: Lebusque comes shooting past me. Some son of a bitch has knocked over the filing cabinet of plans; pieces of paper go flying everywhere. Should I open a gap for him? Let Lebusque win? Is he planning to pull the sprint for me? Can he even do that? If I start thinking, Reilhan will take the curves first and win.

I go past Lebusque; I have to strain for it. Now I'm leading the race again. Fifty meters from the corner. You couldn't tell from looking at me what kind of interests were at stake. I see everything. Here, a sewer grate. I even come up with jokes. My wheel could get caught in the grating. The others making their spurt and me here, immobile, like a forest punished by petrification. Sercu always thinks of things like that too. It has to do with confidence. When everything in you is confident, you can think whatever you like. A gendarme points right. Here's the curve to the right. I lead across the bridge. A gendarme points left. I go left.

And now I find myself at the start of the last straightaway to the finish. The shouting of hundreds of people along the street rolls in and hits me. Then inside me it grows quiet again.

I take a deep breath and sprint.

My sporting career: 1952

I organized a long-jump championship in our yard. The contestants were a girl from my block and myself. Just like in the Olympics, each of us was allowed six attempts. Unlike standard Olympic procedure, however, it was possible for one athlete to win different medals in the same event. And so it came to pass that I actually won gold, silver *and* bronze. In my notebook I wrote: Long jump: 1. T. Krabbé: 2.12 m. 2. T. Krabbé: 2.03 m. 3. T. Krabbé: 1.98 m.

I come up out of the saddle, I clench my teeth. 'Heakk!' I say. Two, three kicks, and my full speed has gone out of my head and into my wheels.

At any given moment, every human being has at his disposal a brief, intense death struggle that doesn't hurt and which lasts twelve seconds. That's the animal sprint. Of all the things that prevent the rider from achieving the speed of light during those twelve seconds, pain is not one.

Sprinting is a frenzy!

Sprints have been lost because feet broke out of toe clips, pedals snapped, handlebars were torn from head tubes, wheels wrenched out from under bikes, tires wrung from rims.

Jesus, I'm going fast. I have to have won this. I'm not shifting down, just like I thought. I really exploded out of there. Maybe I don't even have to kick the whole way. Anyway, I can sit down again.

Holy shit, Tim! You've got it!

I sit. Should I start listening to the cheering? Whatever I do, I'm never going to lose another sprint to Reilhan. But watch out, to my right a wheel is coming up beside me. Well, if you want to call that beside me, that wheel's no further than my bracket. Reilhan.

The wheel moves up. Which means it would be a good idea to draw a little more speed out of my frenzy. The wheel creeps up another five centimeters, then stops at the back of my front wheel. Unh, that was scary for a moment there, but I took care of it. Good work. Now hold onto it.

The twelve seconds are over, my evolution to man is complete. Now the beast falls, I go on. Reilhan's wheel slides up a centimeter, then another. Sprinting goes so slowly, you could replay our sprint with two thimbles on a cheeseboard. Now I can clearly perceive in myself an impossibility to go on, and pain.

He's trying to get by me.

I struggle, he can't do that. The banner at the finish is twelve kicks away. Reilhan slides up three centimeters. So he's going faster than I am. But it's not about who's going faster at a given moment, it's about who gets somewhere first. I'm first in the Tour de Mont Aigoual.

My legs are in a terrible fight to take their turn for the next kick. But it seems like the pain is making me less sure about how you get those kicks out of your frenzy. Reilhan's wheel creeps further.

A biased observer might think that Reilhan and I are neck and neck. The finish line is three kicks away. Reilhan is one centimeter in front. I know that when I'm willing to go to the bottom of every bottom, I'll win. But a great discouragement overpowers me. What did I ever do to deserve the way that wheel keeps moving up? This race was there for me. Sure, I can still win it, but how? It's such a pity. Besides, I can't any more.

No defeatism, Tim. I have to get back to my frenzy to retrieve the kick that will make it turn out all right. Then that's what I'll do. Sprints have changed winners at the most unbelievable moments.

But now something in Reilhan's behavior catches my eye. Very strange: he's changed his hunched posture a bit. As if he's no longer hunching over, but slowly sitting up, spreading his arms like a skydiver in a free fall, sitting up further, raising his arms, his hands above his head.

○

Kilometer 137. Reilhan crosses the line first, I'm second. Roaring and shrieking. The dam of my tiredness bursts. Reilhan sits up straight on his saddle, drops back down, his hands on the bars. We're holding our legs still, we've rolled back out of the noise. Right now I'm a complete rag. Right now I'm a complete rag. I open my eyes and my mouth wide. I get my legs back when they're turning again. I have a black heart pumping powerlessness to all parts of my body. I have to brake, I'm riding between a line of cars and the sidewalk. A punch to the gear lever: forty-three fifteen. I turn, I'm past the cars, past the noise. In front of me is Reilhan. He brakes and turns, real dumb: I have to swerve to avoid him, and almost fall. I cycle on, into the quiet. To the left, a little river; to the right, houses. On a stone wall beside the river, two thirteen-year-old girls are sitting. There's a laundry basket in between them. They're swinging their legs back and forth. I look at them and they look at me. I cycle further; this is how you go to the Causse Noir. We went this way just a while ago. I'm almost out of Meyrueis, I can already see the start of the climb, it's quiet here. Someone comes out of a bakery with a bag in his hand. My head is hanging down, my breathing is deep.

A hand on my shoulder. Kléber.

We turn back together. The gear I'm in is much too heavy. I shift, forty-three nineteen.

'Did you get him?'

'No. Ten centimeters.'

'I was fourth. Lebusque cut me off, the son of a bitch.'

'Ten centimeters.'

We ride. Two girls with a laundry basket. Kléber, I'm a complete rag.

'Did you see it? Today I attacked.'

'Too late.'

'Oh . . .' He looks at me, to see if I really mean it. 'It was tough.'

'Stani . . .' Here, here comes the first breath that I'm completely conscious of. Hucch!! Hucch hucch!

'Stani, you were the strongest.'

Meyrueis. We come back past the line of cars that have been held up here by the end of our race.

The finish line, people, fussing. 'Clear the road!' As if Kléber, Lebusque and I hadn't already swept that road clean for the next half-hour.

Reilhan is standing at the finish line, hanging over his bars. I ride past him, my hand shoots out, I give him a smack on the shoulder. He doesn't react, he's still leaning over. I ride on to my car, try to open it three times, then Stéphan comes along and gives me the key. He hugs me. 'You rode well.' He also gives me back my flat front wheel. I lean against my car.

'Ten centimeters.'

'You rode well.'

I put my bike up against the wall, climb in behind the wheel and look straight ahead.

I'm parked right at the finish, I'll be able to watch the stragglers arrive, I'll note how much later they come in. How many minutes have gone by already? The whole countryside here must be full of dumped riders. I take a drink, I lean on the steering wheel, open my eyes wide, wipe my forehead. I eat a banana, a peach. Another banana.

A knock on the glass. Sauveplane. In his street clothes. I flip up the little window.

'Goddamn it, I thought you were going to get him.'

'Ten centimeters.'

'Not even that! Goddamn it, I thought you had him. But he's fast, Reilhan. Class. I really don't have enough time to train. I climbed off the first time we came through.' He gives me a wink. 'First among the losers!'

Cheering, clapping, from people at the sidewalk cafés. Two riders turn onto the straightaway: Barthélemy and Boutonnet. Six minutes behind. Barthélemy hangs his head and doesn't sprint. Boutonnet comes in fifth. I lean forward on the wheel.

Eight minutes: a group of three is coming in. Sanchez wins the sprint by a length, in front of a rider in a Molteni jersey. Teissonnière rolls out. Teissonnière! I didn't even see whether he had blood on him. Fifteen seconds later, a lone rider comes in: the rider from Cycles Goff. He's back at the line right away, lets his bike fall to the ground and sinks back against the curb. It looks like he's crying, but I don't hear anything. A man rushes over, grabs one of the guy's legs and pushes it in the air. Cycles Goff is staring at the sky. A little boy picks up the fallen bike; another one crouches down next to it: they're pointing out bike parts to each other. Now the rider from Cycles Goff is drinking.

I climb out and take off my cycling gear. I dry off and put on my street clothes. I unpin the number from my jersey and bring it to the race officials at the line. I'm handed two hundred francs. Fifty for the premium at Camprieu, a hundred and fifty for second place.

I see Reilhan's father's car. Reilhan is sitting in the back seat. His mother is on her knees on the front seat, dabbing at his face with a washcloth.

Friends and spectators around the car. Now the speaker moves to the mike and says that Reilhan from Nîmes has won the Tour de Mont Aigoual. Applause. I look at his father: he's biting back a smile. Reilhan comes out of the car, the speaker is holding a bouquet, a young girl is pushed forward by another young girl, the speaker hands her the flowers and she hands them to Reilhan. They kiss. Reilhan raises the bouquet to the crowd. Shouting. Applause.

Do I clap along with them?

No. By applauding I would be saying: Hell, Reilhan, it wasn't that important, it was just good fun. I would be saying: You only beat a part of me, and the rest, what does it care, it applauds you.

But Reilhan has beaten all of me.

He who applauds his victor denies that, and belittles him. Being a good loser is a despicable evasion, an insult to the sporting spirit. All good losers should be barred from practicing a sport.

Reilhan takes one flower from his bouquet and gives it to the girl. Once again he holds his flowers on high. '*Bravo, Poupou.*' The sense of superiority bolstered once again.

I'd like to press him against me, I'd like to lean over that stone wall with him and look at the little river, talk about our adventures. Without masks. I'll tell him that he has great talent, but that, until he turns twenty, he shouldn't win as many races as possible, but gather as much courage as possible.

There's a tap on my shoulder.

'You the one who just came in second?'

'Yeah.'

'You went for it too soon.'

'No.'

'Oh yeah, you couldn't make it, you sprinted like a jackass. Don't try to tell me about sprinting.'

I don't even know this man. 'I'm the kind of rider who—'

'You should have gone later. You'd have eaten him up. That guy who won was laughing himself to death on your wheel for a hundred meters, then he got you. If you'd wait fifty meters . . .'

'Then he'd have jumped.'

'And then you win, because for him that's too early, but not for you. I've got eyes, right? You sprinted like a jackass.'

I'm trapped in the whirlpool of goofy smiles around Reilhan, and suddenly I'm standing next to him. We look at each other. Tense eyes all around us. What do champions like these say to each other at moments like this? Accusations come to mind. But no, what the hell.

'What were you sprinting on?' I ask.

'Sixteen.'

I whistle admiringly, golden boys spurt light. 'I was on my fifteen. Maybe I should have gone to the fourteen.' A grunt job, I admit it openly, and it didn't even work.

Reilhan shrugs and smiles. To him a victory is something he's always had, something that could at most be taken away from him in a race. He's already talking to someone else; he doesn't look any more tired than all those other people around him.

My sleeve is being tugged at. It's that sprinting expert again. 'It was good that you came through the curve first. That was good! But you should have gone for it later!'

I walk on.

145

Cars with riders in them. Teissonnière is leaning against a fender. His wife is working with a bottle and a cloth; she's rubbing it over a red, raw spot that runs down the whole side of his left leg.

'Second?'

'Yeah. Ten centimeters. If you'd been there, one of us would have won. Reilhan didn't have much left. Jesus, man, when I saw you lying there . . .'

'Puncture. Always nasty on the downhill.' He shrugs. 'I've had worse falls.'

I nod. 'Maybe I should have waited before I went for it,' I say.

Lebusque in denims. A nod towards Reilhan. 'Little prick, didn't pull one meter. Not one. That's not racing. Lets me do all the work. And I'm forty-two!'

Lebusque has reached the age of forty-two without ever understanding that Reilhan, for all his wheel-sucking, is more of a racer than he is, no matter how much he pulls.

'Lebusque, today you were the strongest man out there.'

'Did you get me?'

'What?'

He nods in the direction of the Perjuret. 'Did you get why I waited for you? Because I could have left you there, you know that. It was to get that little prick. Why didn't you let me pull the sprint for you? Shithead, I was going to pull the sprint for you.'

'Look out.' I pull him back. Four riders come flying along the curb, sprinting for eleventh place, behind by

146

more than fifteen minutes. Guillaumet makes it, ahead of Petit. Five years of racing have taken me from that sprint to this curb.

I go back to my car, take my bike apart, put it in. Clothes, pump, wheels: I toss it all loose and on top of each other in the trunk. Yanking on his bars, Wolniak wins the sprint for seventeenth place.

I eat an orange, a banana, two sandwiches. The rider from Cycles Goff is sitting on the ground; he has his arms wrapped around his knees and he's staring down.

Half an hour's past. Every few minutes little groups of riders have come in, and the cheering becomes more hilarious each time. I sit behind the wheel and start the engine. Shouting, people are telling me to wait.

A rider's coming in. He rides slowly down the street, passersby pointing him out to one another. It's Despuech, with the sag car behind him. He wanted to finish the Tour de Mont Aigoual.

He sees me.

Despuech's smile after 137 kilometers, seven years later. One eyebrow waggles. I shake my head and hold up two fingers. He nods, he understands. He rides on.

I leave Meyrueis, heading for the Col de Perjuret.

At Salvensac I'm passed by a big car with wheels and frames on the roof, the Reilhans. Reilhan is sitting in the back seat. He half raises his hand, he's looking out in front again, he's gone.

To the left, neat green pastures climb steeply; at the edge of the high plateau, black trees stand waving; to the right, a black-blue sky. On Mont Aigoual it must still be raining.

At the top of the Col de Perjuret I climb out to piss.

My sporting career: 1948
We had a typewriter and sometimes I was allowed to use it. I typed all the numbers. I started with 1 and went up from there. Each number was higher than the one before. My life was all about breaking records.

A NOTE ON THE AUTHOR

Tim Krabbé is a chess as well as a cycling enthusiast and one of Holland's leading writers. His many books include the novels *The Vanishing* (twice filmed, in Holland and the United States) as well as *The Cave* (also filmed), as well as the cycling classic, *The Rider*. He lives in Amsterdam.

Sam Garrett, a former wire-service correspondent, is the translator of *The Cave* by Tim Krabbé, *The Gates of Damascus* by Lieve Joris and *Silent Extras* by Arnon Grunberg.

A NOTE ON THE TYPE

The text of this book is set in Bembo. This type was first used in 1495 by the Venetian printer Aldus Manutius for Cardinal Bembo's *De Aetna*, and was cut for Manutius by Francesco Griffo. It was one of the types used by Claude Garamond (1480–1561) as a model for his Romain de L'Université, and so it was the forerunner of what became standard European type for the following two centuries. Its modern form follows the original types and was designed for Monotype in 1929.